T0159263

THE
LITTLE
HISTORY
OF
ESSEX

THE
LITTLE
HISTORY
OF
ESSEX

JUDITH
WILLIAMS

First published 2017

The History Press
The Mill, Brimscombe Port
Stroud, Gloucestershire, GL5 2QG
www.thehistorypress.co.uk

British Library Cataloguing in Publication Data.
A catalogue record for this book is available from the British Library.

ISBN 978 0 7509 7041 9

Typesetting and origination by The History Press
Printed in Turkey

CONTENTS

	About the Author	6
1	The Beginning of Essex	7
2	Norman Essex: William Takes Over	25
3	Medieval Essex: Sheep, Sheep, Sheep and Cloth	39
4	Tudor Essex: Where Have all our Monasteries Gone?	56
5	Stuart Essex: A Civil War	81
6	Georgian Essex: Rising Fortunes	99
7	Victorian Essex: Ups and Downs	127
8	A New Century: Work and Play	147
9	Two Wars and a Housing Crisis	157
10	Modern Times	174
	Bibliography	184
	Index	187

ABOUT THE AUTHOR

Judith Williams' interest in the history of Essex was sparked when she was a community columnist for local newspapers. She went on to write six history books about Essex, and eventually trained as a tutor of English and history. Judith is currently involved with the Shoeburyness Military Archives and a heritage centre project for the historic Shoeburyness area. She is helping to produce a Victoria County History 'short' for the Southend area. Judith is a member of the Friends of Essex Churches Trust and enjoys church bell ringing. She lives in Southend.

1

THE BEGINNING OF ESSEX

The Essex of 450,000 years ago would be unrecognisable to modern man. The River Thames flowed eastwards above London via the sites of Chelmsford and Colchester, and what is now the River Medway flowed north across 'Essex' towards Clacton.

There is evidence of early man living in the area. For example, 400,000-year-old finds at Clacton – flint chopping tools and a worked wooden staff – have given the name 'Clactonian man' to a whole group of *Homo erectus* people. Chafford Gorge shows evidence of human activity on the banks of the River Thames 200,000 years ago, in a period between ice ages. These were Neanderthals, not modern *Homo sapiens*, and the Essex Field Club paints a vivid picture of these people living below the chalk cliff and making flint tools to kill and prepare tasty meals of the local rhinoceros, bison, mammoth and elephant. Brown bears provided warm clothing and furry blankets.

Fossil remains tell us that hippopotamuses were still living in the area around East Mersea 120,000 years ago. Then, during the most recent ice age, a vast sheet of ice diverted the Thames and the Medway to their current positions. Reindeer and arctic wolves arrived while the hippopotamus died out.

Meltwater gushing from the ice sheet, carrying stones with it, accounts for the large 'erratic' boulders, or sarsen stones, found in Essex. Of more long-term significance were the fertile glacial tills laid down in north-west and central Essex, and the London clay in the south of the county.

When this last ice age ended 10,000 years ago, Britain was joined to the main European landmass. Places like Canvey Island and Foulness Island, although still relatively close to rivers that later became the Thames and the Crouch, would have been 30–50km from the open ocean. Neolithic people walked across from Europe to the area that is now Essex, where they lived by hunting, fishing and gathering nuts and berries. They often occupied sites that are now below sea level, such as near Hullbridge, where many flint tools have been found below the water level. Similarly, numerous broken flints of undoubted human workmanship show three separate Palaeolithic communities living at Purfleet. Evidence of older sea levels can still be seen here, where a forest was submerged beneath the Thames.

The fossiliferous cliffs at Walton-on-the-Naze give further clues to the history of the coast, with layers of clay, Red Crag, brickearth, gravel and volcanic ash. The successive layers show the changing conditions. Around 8,000 years ago a violent tsunami, along with more gradual rises in sea level (as much as 2m every 100 years), filled the area of the North Sea and English Channel with water. Britain became an island, separated from continental Europe, and the long Essex coastline was formed. This coastline, together with the underlying geology and its patterns of rivers and hills, has influenced settlement and land use in Essex ever since.

The result of these geological processes is a county with low hills, undulating valleys and extensive flat land areas around the coast. Chelmsford stands about 30m above sea level, with the land rising to just over 130m west of Saffron Walden. Of the low hills and ridges that interrupt this pattern, the highest is Danbury Hill at 116m.

EARLY ESSEX BOYS AND GIRLS

Neolithic man was living in the Chelmsford area around 6,000 years ago (4000 BC), gradually changing his hunter-gatherer lifestyle into a farming one. There is evidence of communities living in the area of Marks Tey, Kelvedon, Witham and at Tiptree, where there were freshwater lakes. They also lived on the coast, for example at Walton-on-the-Naze, Southchurch and Shoeburyness, and by rivers, such as at Little Chesterford on the River Cam.

Settlers in the area of present-day Springfield built a cursus. This was a huge oval earthwork and its purpose was ... well, no one knows for sure. The monument is a pair of parallel earth banks about 670m long and 40m wide, with surrounding ditches. It is orientated north-east–south-west. Burnt animal bones and pot sherds suggest the site was probably used for ceremonial purposes and burials. The cursus also contains Bronze Age remains (pot fragments, for example) and, therefore, it is likely that it was used over a very long period of time.

Similarly, archaeological work in Mucking, Thurrock, has revealed graves and pits from the Neolithic period, a Bronze Age hill fort, over 100 Iron Age roundhouses, a Roman villa, a Romano-British cemetery and Anglo-Saxon huts.

BRONZE AGE ESSEX (2500–800 BC)

During the Bronze Age, settlements continued to be concentrated around the coast and river valleys. For example, Clacton was still an important site, as were the banks of the River Thames. A wooden oar, known as the Canewdon Paddle, which was found on the south bank of the River Crouch is the earliest example of oars being used in northern Europe.

At this time, the field systems were enlarged as farming became the typical lifestyle. Homes were simple wooden structures built over a platform of brushwood or timber, and permanent tracks began to develop as people regularly walked the same routes. Traders began to bring metal from Europe for working into tools, or to be traded for other goods here in Essex. Also, salt manufacturing began around the coast.

The largest Bronze Age cemetery in Essex is at Ardleigh.

IRON AGE ESSEX

During the Iron Age, people began to settle on the higher ground. They formed themselves into tribes and defended their home territories from other groups and, as the population expanded, land continued to be cleared for planting crops of wheat and barley.

North of the Thames, the Trinovantes tribe dominated, with their main settlement in north-east Essex. Their tribal headquarters was Camulodunum, a fortress of the war god, Camulos, sited about 3 miles from the current town of Colchester, in the area of Gosbecks Farm. This sprawling settlement of huts was defended by a complex series of earth banks and dykes.

A line of hill forts separated the Trinovantes territory from their neighbours, the Catuvellauni. For example, Ambresbury Bank in Epping Forest encloses an area of some 11 acres and was the site of a village for some 350 years (700 BC–AD 50). Nearby Loughton Camp is a similar size, sited on a strategic ridge of high ground, while a third site in this defensive line, Ring Hill at Littlebury, is slightly smaller. Other Iron Age hill forts include those at Norsey Woods, Billericay, Fossets Farm at Southend, Chipping Hill at Witham and at Danbury.

Elsewhere in east Essex, where there are no hills, Iron Age people defended their village huts with ditches and huge earth banks called ramparts. Examples of these are at Asheldham and at Shoeburyness.

In the late Iron Age, salt production along the coast increased and seawater was evaporated in large quantities for generations. The activity resulted in the formation of 'red hills', which can still be found around the coast from Canvey Island to Harwich. Red hills were large mounds (with bases up to 115m in diameter) of waste materials produced by the salt-making industry, mostly broken pottery and ash. The red colour comes from the continued action of intense heat on the pots and surrounding soil. Excavation of some of these hills has revealed the mechanics of the industry: hearths, flues and clay-lined pits where the salt water settled.

During the late Iron Age the tribal leader Cunobelin led his Catuvellauni tribe in an invasion of Essex from the St Alban's area. They defeated the Trinovantes and took over Camulodunum. However, Cunobelin was not in charge for long. The Romans decided that Britain would make a prestigious addition to the Roman Empire and they already knew that Essex would provide rich pickings. The empire had been trading peacefully with Essex for several years, exchanging pottery and oil from the continent with salt, food (including oysters) and well-trained hunting dogs.

Addedomaros was the last leader of the Trinovantes, and it could be he that was buried in the important Lexden tumulus, close to Gosbecks. Alternatively, the mound could contain the remains of the invading Cunobelin. Certainly, a wealthy noble was cremated and then buried there with a mix of Celtic and Roman artefacts.

ROMAN ESSEX – COLCHESTER IS THE PLACE TO BE!

In AD 43, 50,000 Roman soldiers disembarked in Kent and set off immediately for Camulodunum. Having crossed the Thames into Essex, they waited for Emperor Claudius himself to arrive with additional troops and some elephants with which to intimidate the natives.

While the Romans marched into Camulodunum, Caratacus (Cunobelin's son, who was then ruling the area) escaped from the back entrance with a few men. However, Caratacus was soon caught, taken to Rome and paraded through the streets to represent the defeated Britons. The Romans immediately began constructing a legionary fortress about 3 miles north-east of the Iron Age capital at Camulodunum. It was the first time that bricks and mortar had been used in Britain, and vast quantities of timber, sand, gravel and clay were brought from the surrounding area to create a huge, regimented settlement.

Within five years, confident in their control of the locals, the Romans adapted their fortress at Camulodunum into a colony for military veterans and named it Colonia Claudia, after the emperor. The Roman administrators converted the barrack blocks into homes and allocated plots of land to retired soldiers, displacing the Britons. The Romans – in fact, a mix of recruits, mercenaries and slaves from Gaul, Hungary, Germany and North Africa – were here to stay and, for a short time, Colonia Claudia was the capital city of Britain. They built public halls, shops, baths and three theatres. An imposing monumental arch replaced the military gate at the western entrance to the colony. When the Emperor Claudius died in AD 54, the loyal colonials in their thriving new city constructed an impressive temple dedicated to him.

ROMAN ROADS

The earliest roads built by the Romans were tracks for moving soldiers and equipment around quickly. Later, a few of these became major routes which were used for trade and transport. Three main roads ran through Essex:

1 The road between London and Colchester. This road passed through Caesaromagus (Chelmsford) and Canonium (Kelvedon), and then continued on to Ipswich.
2 Stane Street, which ran east to west between Colchester and the west Essex boundary. This road passed through settlements where Braintree and Great Dunmow now stand, following the River Roding for part of its course.
3 Ermine Street, which ran between London and a walled Roman town just north of the present town of Great Chesterford.

The Bartlow Hills, Romano-British burial barrows.

BARTLOW HILLS

Around 1 BC to AD 100, some wealthy Britons built seven huge burial mounds (barrows), largely of local chalk. Now known as the Bartlow Hills, these barrows were in Essex until boundary changes in 1990 transferred them to Cambridgeshire. Their existence shows an overlap of British and Roman culture as barrows were popular pre-Roman burial features, although the conical shape of the Bartlow Hills is distinctively Roman.

Whoever was buried here was very wealthy as their cremated bones were surrounded by food, drink and expensive imported pottery, glass and decorated bronze. The tombs also contained wooden chests, folding iron chairs, flowers, blood, milk and wine mixed with honey, all associated with feasting and sacrificial offerings. The mourners lit an oil lamp at the centre of each mound and left it there to burn while they sealed up the entrances to the barrows. Most of the artefacts discovered here during Victorian excavations were entrusted to the safekeeping of Easton Lodge, but all the artefacts, along with most of the Elizabethan lodge itself, were lost in a fire in 1847.

Today, the three remaining barrows (now 14m high but originally nearer 30m) are the largest barrows in Britain after Silbury Hill.

BOUDICCA

Boudicca became the leader of the Iceni tribe of Britons when her husband died in AD 59. The Iceni lived in Suffolk, Norfolk and into Cambridgeshire, and had had a peaceful trading relationship with the new Roman settlers. However, the Roman commanders decided that a female leader was no leader at all. They seized property belonging to Iceni nobles, flogged Boudicca herself and raped her daughters, the two princesses.

Understandably enraged, Boudicca mustered her Iceni troops. They were joined by some Trinovantes men, who were also unhappy at their treatment by the Romans. These rebels followed Boudicca down to Colonia Claudia where they attacked the undefended town (the soldiers were away suppressing Anglesey) with their full force.

The townspeople crowded into the new Temple of Claudius, hoping to hold out until Roman reinforcements could protect them. However, Boudicca and her forces set fire to the town and the temple, roasting everyone inside. They continued on to London and St Albans, devastating land and property as they went. Over 70,000 people died. Finally, a Roman force, marching back from the north, met the Britons somewhere in the Midlands and slaughtered them all. Boudicca is thought to have poisoned her daughters and herself rather than die at Roman hands.

After the revolt, the Romans reasserted their power at Colchester with a new city wall. The reconstructed Temple of Claudius was enclosed by a massive arcade (a covered walkway over 8m high and 122m long), the largest in Britain.

By AD 200, the inhabitants of Colchester were enjoying decorated mosaic floors with underfloor heating in their comfortable town houses. The busy trading town could now boast a chariot-racing circus, a public water supply and a major industrial complex for the manufacture of pottery, glass and metalware. Several of the wealthiest citizens had moved out of the town into country villas.

However, Boudicca was not forgotten and across the rest of the county, a series of forts appeared to deter further rebellions – for example, at Great Chesterford and Caesaromagus (Chelmsford).

THE SAXON SHORE
The Romans constructed a series of nine forts along the east coast of Britain to deter repeated raids from Saxons and Vikings, and protect trade routes. The fort at Bradwell-on-Sea, named Ythanceaster by the Romans and later called Othona, was built between AD 280 and 290. Walls of over 4m thick enclosed an area of 2 hectares around the fort.

The one remaining contemporary record of the fort tells us that it was manned by the '*numerus*'. These men were a 300-strong infantry unit of the *limitanei*, or border forces. They operated as frontier guards and customs police, and prevented small-scale raids. There may have been a similar fort at Shoeburyness that, due to rising sea levels, has since disappeared beneath the sea.

CAESAROMAGUS
Ten years after Boudicca's revolt, the fort just south of the River Cam, on the road to Colchester, was no longer a military centre. A market town had developed on the site: Caesaromagus, or 'Caesar's Market', centred on what we now know as Moulsham Street. Farmers, who grew cereals in a regular grid pattern of fields, came to exchange their

produce for pottery, metalware, household equipment and decorative items made of animal bone and horn.

The original timber fort was soon extended with baths and a religious sector. From AD 120, an official overnight stop, a *mansio*, replaced a smaller 'road station' at this convenient location. It was a day's march from both London and Colchester. The *mansio* offered accommodation to Roman officials passing through the town, with wagons and fresh horses available. Travellers could take advantage of the public baths and sauna (*laconium*), and conduct business in the administrative offices.

Narrow homes and commercial premises were built facing onto the main road. Their construction was a timber frame with wattle and daub infill, clay floors and a thatched roof. They comprised two or three rooms with a corridor on one side.

The growing town strengthened its defences between AD 160 and 175 with earth banks. However, fifty years later,

Green Man, St John's Church, Little Leighs.

these were flattened to allow the expansion of the town in the form of more houses, shops and public buildings.

In the early AD 300s, the inhabitants built an octagonal temple on the edge of the settlement, close to what is now the Baddow Road roundabout. Soon after the temple was built, however, a fire destroyed several buildings in the town. The sporadic way in which these were rebuilt or replaced suggests a declining, rather than expanding town at this time. When the Romans withdrew from Britain in the early fifth century, new settlers did not keep the bridge over the Cam and Chelmer in good repair. Therefore, travellers on the road from London to Colchester preferred the route via Writtle, and Chelmsford itself lost importance.

THE KINGDOM OF THE EAST SAXONS

The Roman Empire withdrew direct control of Britain around AD 400, leaving the country open to settlement by Angles and Saxons from north Germany. There is little evidence that these new settlers had to fight for their new homes and, in many cases, they lived peaceably alongside the Romano-British population. They sailed and rowed across the English Channel and North Sea, coming ashore on England's east coast and making new homes there.

These new homes were often built directly on top of abandoned Romano-British buildings: it was easier to throw up a wattle and daub, thatched hut than to repair stone walls. The Saxons lived in extended family groups. They were farmers who cleared forests to expand their fields, and they grazed sheep on the marshy fringes of the county and set fish traps in the Blackwater, Colne and Stour estuaries, as well as on the River Lea. The salt industry on the coast between Maldon and the Stour was still thriving.

Saxon influence can still be found across the county in village names and in the patterns of field boundaries, around which the narrow Saxon trackways twisted and

turned. They built banks and ditches in Epping Forest and the Strood Causeway at Mersea.

SAXON GOVERNMENT AND ADMINISTRATION

Saxon tribal groups gradually amalgamated to form Essex, the Kingdom of the East Saxons under one tribal chief or 'king' by AD 500. The first recorded king was Aescwine, who was on the throne in 527. However, the King of Essex often found himself having to pay tribute to the more powerful overlords of Kent, Anglia or Mercia.

The Saxons imposed their own administrative system on the land, defining areas within official boundaries called 'hundreds'. Essex was divided into nineteen of these. A hundred is an area capable of supporting 100 families (although the exact definition of 'hundred' is not proven and it may instead refer to a specific acreage of productive land).

The 'Hundred Men' were the chiefs of their tribes, who met together in the main village of each hundred to discuss

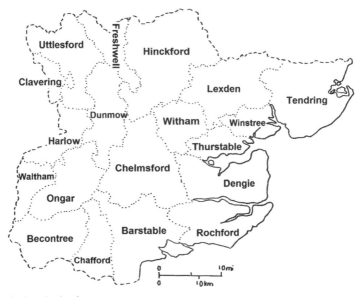

The hundreds of Essex.

legal and taxation matters and to co-operate on the running of the Kingdom of Essex. The term 'Hundred Men' became corrupted into 'ealdormen' and later 'aldermen'. The last Saxon King of Essex was Sigered, who allowed the territory to become annexed to Wessex in AD 825.

ST CEDD AT ST PETER'S ON THE WALL

Mellitus became Bishop of London around AD 604, with a mission to convert the locals to Christianity. The bishopric of London included Essex, and Mellitus was successful in converting the Saxon King Saebert. Saebert, in turn, convinced the Hundred Men of Essex to update their pagan beliefs. However, after the death of King Saebert in AD 616, Mellitus was driven out by locals who were presumably fed up with the constraints of following Christian 'rules'. Essex reverted to paganism.

However, King Sigebert II (reigned *c.* 653–60) became a Christian and invited the monk, Cedd, to bring the Christian message to the people of Essex. Sigebert may indeed have been a good religious man, or it could be that he saw Christianity as a useful tool with which to control his people. Cedd accepted the invitation and sailed down from Northumberland to become the new Bishop of London. He built a chapel on the foundations of the Roman fort on Bradwell seawall. It is thanks to the Romans importing and leaving building stone in the area that Cedd's church still stands.

Cedd also founded minsters (mother churches) at Barking, Tilbury, Great Wakering and Southminster. Their locations evidence the seaborne activity around the Essex coast at the time. Unfortunately for Cedd, he caught the plague on a visit to Lastingham in his native North Yorkshire (then in the Saxon Kingdom of Northumbria), and he died. Unfortunate, too, for the faithful monks who he had recruited in Essex to help him with spreading his gospel. A party of thirty Essex monks travelled to

Lastingham to pay their respects at Cedd's funeral, where they also caught the plague and twenty-nine of them died.

However, Cedd had done enough to kickstart the spread of Christianity and he was later made a saint. Local Saxon chiefs encouraged the building of a church in every village: probably just a basic hut from which a priest could preach, and by necessity mostly built of wood. This new common religion helped to cement a cohesive society that was easier for the chiefs to control and indoctrinate via preaching.

Mellitus also became a saint and he is depicted in stonework and stained-glass windows in many Essex churches today.

St Andrew's at Greensted is the oldest wooden church in the world and the oldest stave-built building in Europe, with timbers dating to 1060. The church has always been thought to be of Saxon origin, but it is possible, of course, that the Normans built the church with aged timber.

St Andrew's, Greensted, as it was before the renovations in 1848.

A SAXON PRINCE
The so-called Saxon 'Prince of Prittlewell' died around 650. His tomb (1 mile north of present-day Southend town centre) had been carefully prepared. Those in charge dug a deep pit and lined it with wooden stakes. They laid out the body and carefully arranged his possessions: luxury imported glass vases, gaming sets, musical instruments and tools. On his body, they placed a golden belt buckle and laid two small crosses of beaten gold on his eyelids. These crosses suggest this wealthy individual may have been either King Saebert or Sigebert himself. We will probably never know.

BARKING ABBEY
Erkenwald, later to become Bishop of London and a saint, founded a monastery at Barking in 666 for his sister, Ethelburga, who became the first abbess. The abbey has had an exciting history. For example, in 870 a mob of Danes broke into the abbey, herded the virgin sisters into the chapel and burnt them all to death.

The buildings were more or less abandoned for a century until King Edgar allowed Wulfhilda to become the new abbess. Wulfhilda had refused to marry Edgar and he had almost forced himself on her, repenting at the last moment and allowing her to become a nun instead. The buildings were repaired and restored and Barking's wealth continued to grow. The abbey came to own land as far afield as Warley, Ingatestone, Roding, Tollesbury and Wigborough, and the nuns were allowed many privileges denied to others, such as the right to take hares and collect firewood from the king's forests.

BATTLES WITH THE DANES

In 917, the Wessex King Edward the Elder, son of Alfred the Great, forced out some Danes who had been occupying Colchester. Edward arranged for the town's walls to be repaired to help it resist further attacks by the Danes. He probably knew the town by its new Saxon name: Colneceaster: the fortress on the River Colne.

Aethelred the Unready was king of England from 978 to 1016. His reign saw three significant battles on the Essex coast to repel Viking raids. These Viking expeditions to England were usually led by the Danish kings, but they were composed of warriors from all over Scandinavia.

THE BATTLE OF BENFLEET, 894
(SAXONS V. DANES)

In 894, a community of Danes had camped at South Benfleet, mooring their longships in the creek. While many of the men went off to hunt for food, a party of Saxons, led by King Alfred's son, attacked the camp. They successfully captured several women and children, including the wife and children of Haesten, the Danish leader. Escaping Danes jumped into their boats and fled to Shoeburyness where they made camp within an old Iron Age rampart. However, they soon moved on to a larger camp at Mersea.

Alfred was not an unreasonable man, and Haesten's family were returned to him as part of the post-battle negotiations over land ownership.

BATTLE OF MALDON 991 (BYRHTNOTH V. VIKINGS)

Throughout 991, East Anglia was continually plagued by Viking raids. The people of Maldon heard that the enemy were making their way down to the Blackwater but were relieved that the Saxon hero Byrhtnoth was bringing his army there to ward off the invasion. Byrhtnoth had an excellent track record at defeating Vikings but, although standing over 6ft tall, he was over 60 years old by 991 and was described in the *Anglo-Saxon Chronicle* as having 'swan white' hair.

The Vikings pulled their boats onto Northey Island and massed on the shore there as Byrhtnoth drew up his troops on the mainland on 10 August 991. There were some 4,000–6,000 men on each side. All were heavily armed and ready to fight. As the tide receded, Byrhtnoth allowed the Viking warriors to surge across the causeway hoping, no doubt, for a swift and decisive battle. Byrhtnoth was unlucky that day and was killed – some say by a single blow from a Viking sword; others that it took three Vikings to cut him down. His death caused panic among the Saxons and some of them deserted the battlefield. Those who were left were no match for the invaders and all were killed. Despite their victory, the remaining Vikings were all exhausted and many wounded. They limped back to their ships, rather than attack Maldon itself.

Although he died, Byrhtnoth was proclaimed a hero. An epic poem was written about the battle, most of which has survived until the present day, ensuring Byrhtnoth's fame for posterity.

King Ethelred must have despaired of ever ridding his country of the Vikings, and he negotiated a deal with them: a payment of 10,000 Roman pounds (3,300kg) of silver to stop the attacks. This was the first known payment of what became known as the '*Danegeld*' – effectively protection money. The Vikings were delighted with the arrangement and began to use the same policy of extortion elsewhere in Britain. In fact, more Anglo-Saxon coins from this period have been found in Denmark than in England, perhaps not surprising as the *Danegeld* area stretched from Essex to North Yorkshire.

Maldon honoured Byrhtnoth in the eighteenth century with a statue on All Saints Church, and again in 2006 when they erected a 9ft statue of the hero in Promenade Park.

BATTLE OF ASHINGDON, 1016 (EDMUND IRONSIDE V. CANUTE)

When King Aethelred died in 1016, the Danish King Canute saw an opportunity to seize control of the whole of England. He led his army against Edmund Ironside (Aethelred's son) at Ashingdon (Assendun) near Rochford on 18 October 1016. Eadric of Mercia had promised to support Edmund, but early in the day he deliberately led his followers away from the battle. This loss of a vital section of his army led to Edmund's defeat and he was forced to flee for his life.

After the battle, Canute had a church built on the top of Ashingdon hill to commemorate all those who had died, both English and Danes. He could afford to be generous – he was now king of all England – but he was no fool and no fan of traitors, so he saw to it that Eadric of Mercia was executed. The first priest at Ashingdon was Stigand, who later became Archbishop of Canterbury.

Canute's two sons came to rule England in due course. However, it was only twenty-six years after the Battle of Ashingdon in 1042 that Canute's stepson, the Saxon Edward the Confessor was declared king. The old Saxon ways were restored.

On a visit to Normandy in 1046, Edward the Confessor granted West Mersea and part of Fingringhoe to the Abbey of St Ouen in France. Hence, West Mersea Priory became the first priory in Essex.

It was widely reported that on his deathbed, Edward handed control of England to his friend Harold Godwin. Harold became the last Saxon king. As Earl of Essex and owner of the manor of Waltham, Harold rebuilt the church at Waltham on a larger scale and set up a college of canons to serve the local community. It was here that he prayed on 10 October 1066 before marching south to meet William the Conqueror's forces at Hastings on 14 October.

2

NORMAN ESSEX:
WILLIAM TAKES OVER

In 1066, William of Normandy battled and defeated Harold Godwin at Hastings. Harold's body may have been brought to Waltham Abbey for burial. After the battle, William came to live with the nuns at Barking Abbey while his new castle at Tower Hill was being built. Later, in 1076, he ordered a royal fortress to be built at Colchester, with a new keep on the foundations of the Roman temple. The building and later guardianship of the castle was entrusted to Eudo Dapifer – Eudo the Steward.

The Normans took over an Essex that comprised 440 villages and hamlets. The population was some 14,500 people, with over a quarter of them living in the thirty largest villages. Most villages had fewer than twenty households. By 1086, the three largest settlements were Colchester borough, with 448 households, Barking, with 236 households, and Maldon, with 223 households. However, apart from those three, more people were living in north-west Essex than in the south or east of the county.

Even at this early stage, the most rapid population growth appears to have been on the borders of London. West Ham, for example, had sixteen cottagers in 1066

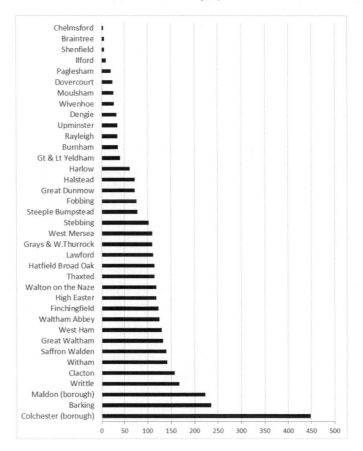

Populations at Domesday (1086): a selection to show comparative sizes.

but twenty years later had seventy-nine. Some of these new residents must have been incomers, perhaps displaced from other villages. Or had they been brought in for specific work, such as clearing the dense forest that dominated central west Essex? Certainly, there was a lot of work to do there at the nine watermills on the Lea. The Normans, with their families, probably numbered about 300 individuals.

WHO'S WHO IN NORMAN ESSEX?

Many pre-Conquest landowners were dispossessed by the Norman invaders. It is thought that the Saxons of Essex lost more land to the Normans than in any other county, and more freemen lost their status. However, William's friend Robert FitzWimarc, whose principle seat was at Clavering, not only kept his property but was also awarded more.

The new Norman landholders were:

> The king's brother Odo, Bishop of Bayeux – received thirty-nine manors in Essex.
>
> Geoffrey de Magnaville (or Mandeville) – received forty Essex manors.
>
> Eudo Dapifer, son of the king's steward – twenty-five manors in Essex.
>
> Eustace, Earl of Boulogne – received over twenty manors.
>
> William, Earl of Warren – more than forty manors in Essex and elsewhere.
>
> Suene of Essex, FitzWimarc's son – fifty-three manors in Essex.
>
> Aubrey de Vere – held the barony of Chenesitun (Kensington) and land in Middlesex, Cambridgeshire, Huntingdon and Suffolk, but he made his seat at Hedingham in Essex.
>
> Robert Gernon (or Grenon), a great warrior – had the large barony of Stansted, and his successor took the name of Montfichet.
>
> Ralph Baynard, one of the king's attendants – had twenty-five lordships in Essex and many in other counties.
>
> Ralph/Ranulph Peverel, a noble Norman who married William the Conqueror's Saxon concubine – had many lordships in Essex, although his chief barony was at Nottingham.

To retain this wealth for their descendants, these lords and barons made careful marriages. Aubrey de Vere, for example, married Beatrice who was the half-sister of King William. Eudo Dapifer's daughter was married off to Geoffrey Mandeville's son. Their grandson (also Geoffrey Mandeville) married the granddaughter of Aubrey de

Vere (Rohese). Meanwhile, the third Aubrey de Vere, nicknamed 'Aubrey the Grim', married the great-grand-daughter of Suene, Agnes. At the time of this marriage, 'Aubrey the Grim' was aged about 40 while Agnes was 10 years old.

THE EARLS OF ESSEX – GEOFFREY DE MANDEVILLE

Geoffrey de Mandeville was one of the ten wealthiest Normans and he became Constable of the Tower, a very prestigious position. His estates included the valuable Walden and Great Waltham. When Geoffrey died around 1100, his son William inherited both the estates and the responsibilities. However, William allowed an important prisoner to escape from the Tower of London and had to forfeit one-third of his land as a punishment.

It was William's son, the second Geoffrey de Mandeville, who became the first Earl of Essex. Historian J. Round has described this Geoffrey as 'the most perfect and typical presentment of the feudal and anarchic spirit that stamps the reign of Stephen' – by which he means Geoffrey liked a good argument. He spent a great deal of his life attempting to reclaim his father's estates and then to hold on to them.

Initially, Geoffrey declared his support for the new King Stephen, and much of the property was returned to him, along with the title of Earl of Essex. But Stephen's cousin Matilda claimed that the throne of England was hers. When Stephen was captured, Geoffrey renounced him and declared support for Matilda. Matilda forgave him the large debts his father had incurred to the Crown, returned his land and appointed him Sheriff of Essex and Hertfordshire.

Less than a year later, Stephen had reclaimed the throne. Geoffrey was quick to announce his support, but Stephen was no fool and he arrested Geoffrey in 1143, confiscated his castles at Pleshey and Walden, excommunicated him and threatened to execute him.

Geoffrey was not standing for this and he led his supporters to Ramsay Abbey in Cambridgeshire where he threw out the monks and took over. He used the abbey as his headquarters while he lived as an outlaw and plotted against Stephen. Eventually he ambushed the king in 1144, but Geoffrey was killed by an arrow. As he was still excommunicated when he died, Geoffrey could not receive a Christian burial. His body was wrapped in lead and, legend says, it was hung up in a tree. Later, Geoffrey's son, the 2nd Earl of Essex, arranged a proper burial for him in the Temple Church in London and an effigy was placed over the tomb.

THE EARLS OF OXFORD – THE DE VERES

Aubrey de Vere probably came over to England with William the Conqueror, where he was given land in nine counties. His main property was at Hedingham in Essex. When one of Aubrey's sons died young, he founded a priory at Earls Colne which became the mausoleum for the family.

The second Aubrey de Vere began to build a castle at Hedingham with a massive keep (now the best-preserved Norman keep in the United Kingdom). The castle was completed by his son, the third Aubrey de Vere. This Aubrey was given the title of Earl of Oxford, which title the de Vere family retained for twenty generations.

The de Veres acquired the nickname 'the fighting de Veres' for their enthusiastic actions in the wars. There were de Veres on the Crusades, in the Barons' Wars, at Crecy, Poitiers, Agincourt and the Wars of the Roses. They were friends of King Stephen, Richard II and Edward VI. They were involved in Anne Boleyn's coronation and also her execution, and a de Vere carried the crown at Elizabeth I's coronation.

When not fighting, the de Veres were local benefactors. For example, at Earls Colne and Castle Hedingham churches, the de Vere symbols, a five-pointed star and a boar, can be seen inside and out.

A NORMAN INVADER'S HOME IS HIS ...

The *Domesday Book*, King William's survey of Britain, tells us that there were 440 distinct settlements in Essex by 1086. Colchester had the largest, with a population of some 2,500 people. By this time, ninety pre-Conquest landowners of Essex had been deprived of their lands and Essex was especially tyrannised by Norman barons, who constructed castles on their estates for personal security and to awe their dependent vassals.

There were eight baronial castles:

Canfield and Hedingham, belonging to the de Veres, Earls of Oxford.

Clavering and Rayleigh, belonging to Suene.

Ongar, belonging to Richard de Lucy.

Pleshey, a large motte and bailey castle built by Geoffrey de Mandeville.

Stansted Mountfitchet, belonging to de Montfichet.

Walden, built by Geoffrey de Mandeville.

The men who built and lived in the castles were powerful individuals, responsible for maintaining law and order on their estates and ensuring the king's taxes were collected. Living a privileged life, each 'lord' would have enjoyed venison from his hunting park, mutton, pork and beef from farm animals. Some, such as Suene at his well-endowed estates at Rayleigh and Clavering, indulged in wine from their own vineyards and honey from their beehives.

Saxons lived outside the castle bounds in the villages. Their time was spent farming wheat and barley and keeping sheep and pigs. There were 46,000 sheep living in Essex in 1086, probably mostly on the coastal marshes, providing mutton, wool and milk for cheese. Oxen were used for ploughing the land. The villagers' work supported the lord of the manor, his family and retainers, as well as their own families. Several families would have worked at the twenty-eight fisheries listed in the *Domesday* survey.

COLCHESTER CASTLE

William I commissioned a castle to be built at Colchester and it was completed around 1076 by Eudo Dapifer, who also founded St John's Abbey and St Mary Magdalen's Hospital in Colchester. An obituary said that Eudo 'eased the oppressed, restrained the insolent, and pleased all'.

It was convenient to use the base of the former Roman temple as a foundation for the castle keep. This influenced the size of the keep, and so it became the largest Norman keep in England. Eudo built the castle of rubble, stone and Roman tile, and acted as its custodian for his lifetime.

Colchester town received its first royal charter from King Richard I in 1189, which allowed its citizens some rights of self-governance, and the Hythe Port was established nearby before 1200. The purpose of the castle was to subdue and control the local population and also to assist in the defence of the east coast against raids from Scandinavia. However, the first military action it saw was when King John besieged the castle in 1216 during his battles with the barons.

EARLY CHELMSFORD

At the time of the *Domesday* survey (1086) Chelmsford was a tiny hamlet with only four households. The manor belonged to the Bishop of London. The separate village of Moulsham was owned by Westminster Abbey and boasted eleven households, while the two manors in Springfield (Robert Gernon and Ranulph Peverel) supported thirty-one households. In comparison, Writtle had 178 households and was the second wealthiest town in the county (after Colchester). The valuable manors of Great and Little Waltham together had 156 homes.

In 1100 the Bishop of London, Maurice, built a bridge across the River Can. As a result, traffic which used to travel through Writtle now diverted through Chelmsford. With the traffic of pedestrians, carts and wagons came prosperity and in 1215, the growing settlement of Chelmsford became the county town of Essex.

Ruins of St Botolph's Priory, Colchester.

RELIGIOUS HOUSES

At the time of the Norman invasion, there were only three religious houses in Essex: Waltham Holy Cross (then a 'college'), Barking Abbey and West Mersea Priory. Blessed with property and wealth, the Norman barons were keen to perpetuate their good fortune in the next life by founding religious houses for the benefit of their souls.

By 1200, Essex boasted twenty-seven monasteries, abbeys, priories and nunneries. They were set up and endowed with land and properties by Norman lords so that the monks and nuns would pray for the souls of the founders and their families. Norman influences can be seen, for example, in the solidly built churches at Castle Hedingham, Felsted, Heybridge, Stambourne and Great Tey. Norman round-towered churches can be found at Bardfield Saling, Broomfield, Great Leighs Lamarsh, Pentlow and South Ockendon.

WALTHAM ABBEY REVITALISED

In 1177, Henry II, as part of his penitence for the murder of Thomas Becket, re-founded Harold's college at Waltham as a priory of Augustinian canons. In 1184, Henry raised it to the status of an abbey, with an abbot, a prior and twenty-four canons. The abbey was answerable directly to the king, rather than the bishop (this status as a 'royal peculiar' was enjoyed by Waltham until 1865), and Waltham Abbey became the most important of all the Augustinian houses in England. It became a favourite place for many kings, both for religious reasons and as a base for hunting in the Essex forests.

The abbey became extremely wealthy from donations of money and property. However, there were constant disputes with the townspeople. For example, arguments arose over pasturing cattle and rumours about the monks 'undue intimacy' with the nuns of Cheshunt.

A CHARTER FOR MALDON

Maldon was the site of one of the royal mints from 958 to around 1100, issuing coins for the late Saxon and early Norman kings. It was awarded a borough charter by Henry II in 1171, stating the town's rights and privileges as well as defining its borders and detailing its duty to provide a warhorse and a ship for the monarch 'when necessary'. The presence of three churches in the town, All Saints, St Peter's and St Mary's, show its importance. Only Maldon and Colchester have more than one medieval church.

THE DUNMOW FLITCH

The Dunmow Flitch ceremony is thought to date back to 1104. It was begun by Lady Juga Baynard at Little Dunmow. The tradition is that any newly married couple who had lived in complete harmony for at least one year and a day could apply to the prior at Little Dunmow. If their claim was found to be true, the prior would give them a whole side of bacon. By the fourteenth century, fame of the Dunmow Flitch Trials had spread and an annual ceremony began in its new location at Great Dunmow.

THE KNIGHTS TEMPLAR AND KNIGHTS HOSPITALLERS

Grants of property made for the support of the Knights Templar and Hospitallers in Essex considerably outnumbered those in any other county. In fact, the chief house of the hospital at Clerkenwell was itself founded by an Essex man, Jordan Briset, probably early in the reign of King Stephen.

Cressing Temple was given to the Knights Templar in 1137. Today it is known for its Grade I listed barley and wheat barns, built in the thirteenth century; they are among the oldest timber barns and a very few surviving Templar buildings in England.

The town and round church of Little Maplestead were granted to the Knights Hospitallers (the Order of St John of Jerusalem) by Juliana Dosnel around 1170, to be their headquarters in the area. In Henry VIII's 1535 Survey, the possessions of the Hospitallers in Essex, including those which had previously belonged to the Templars, were valued at over £432 a year. The order was dissolved in 1540.

St John's, Little Maplestead. This church belonged to the Knights Hospitallers.

MAGNA CARTA – BIG CHARTER

King John was fond of Essex. He kept at least three hunting lodges (small royal residences) here: one at Writtle, one at Benfleet and one at Thundersley. John gave land at Hadleigh to Hubert de Burgh, his chief minister.

Robert Fitzwalter of Little Dunmow was a powerful man. He was wealthy and influential. But Robert was not happy with how King John was managing the country. Taxation and the responsibilities of the barons were becoming increasingly burdensome. He had already clashed with John over the king's threat to execute Geoffrey Mandeville, 2nd Earl of Essex. In 1212, Robert was accused of plotting against John and had fled to France. There were rumours that John had tried to seduce Robert's daughter, Matilda.

Early in November 1214, King John stayed in Colchester for two days, probably at the castle. Soon afterwards, Robert was at the forefront of rousing his fellow Essex worthies to challenge the king. He enlisted the support of Richard de Montfichet, Sheriff of Essex, Geoffrey de Mandeville of Pleshey, William de Lanvallei, the governor of Colchester Castle, and Robert de Vere of Castle Hedingham. These barons were then joined by twenty others from across England to draw up a list of demands in the form of a charter – Magna Carta – and to oversee its subsequent enforcement.

Robert was named as the leader of the rebellious barons. Although most of the twenty-five lords were from the north and east of England, Essex had a huge concentration of power and influence. History records that King John signed the document in June 1215 at Runnymede near Windsor, land owned by Essex man, Richard de Montfichet. However, John had little intention of allowing the barons their demands and Essex suffered in the unrest that followed – the Barons' War.

Ralph, the abbot of Coggeshall Abbey, kept written accounts of the events. He tells us that John sent troops to seize Hedingham and Pleshey castles. He ransacked Colchester Castle and completely destroyed Stansted Mountfitchet Castle. On Christmas Day 1215, John's soldiers attacked Tilty Abbey, looting the church of its valuables, and killing several monks. Robert Fitzwalter was personally active in these conflicts and was taken prisoner at the Battle of Lincoln.

Chronicler Matthew Paris wrote on Robert Fitzwalter's death in 1235, 'He could match any earl in England: valiant in arms, spirited and illustrious ... generous, surrounded by a multitude of powerful blood relatives and strengthened by numerous relatives in marriage.' More recent reflections, however, have labelled his leadership as 'incompetent'. Robert was buried in front of the altar at Dunmow Priory.

Geoffrey de Mandeville had been allocated the stewardship of Essex in Magna Carta, although he was killed in a tournament just a year later. Interestingly, his widow married Hubert de Burgh who had been on the side of the king during the dispute (although she died only weeks after the wedding).

HADLEIGH CASTLE

Hubert de Burgh was a trusted follower of King John and was the custodian of two important royal castles at Windsor and Dover. He was given land at Hadleigh, Essex, to build a castle overlooking the Thames and his castle here was completed in 1230. Hubert was effectively ruler of England during Henry III's childhood, but his successful career came to an end after quarrels with the king in 1239 and he was forced to return his lands, including Hadleigh. After that, the castle belonged to the Crown, but it was little used until

Edward III made substantial improvements and refortified it with a new barbican and approach road. However, the castle never saw military service.

* * *

The formidable fortresses mentioned in this chapter, once the symbols of Norman power in Essex, have now all but disappeared, save for some mounds of earth, outlines of baileys and a few remaining stones.

3

MEDIEVAL ESSEX: SHEEP, SHEEP, SHEEP AND CLOTH

THE MEDIEVAL LIFESTYLE

By 1200, most Essex people were involved in the manorial feudal system. The lord lived in the relatively vast manor house, holding court and demanding service from the peasants in return for allowing them the security of working on his land. Daily routines for the peasants usually involved tending crops and husbanding animals. They cleared vegetation and levelled the ground to provide more agricultural land. Lime trees, which grow on fertile soil, almost disappeared in the south-east of the county, while oak, elm, hornbeam and beech were managed as crops.

Henry II (1133–89) repudiated King Stephen's leniency on forest laws and declared all of Essex to be royal forest and the whole county was under forest law until 1204. King John began to identify specific areas of parkland designated as royal hunting land and distinct hunting forests emerged, such as Epping Forest, Waltham Forest, Hainault Forest and Rayleigh Park, all comprising areas of both open ground and woodland. Forests were attached to each of the Crown estates at Havering, Writtle and Colchester. Within these areas, villagers were not allowed to hunt wildlife, collect wood or graze pigs. Occasionally, the king granted rights to individuals or groups; for example, the monks of Wix were allowed to keep a pack of dogs to hunt hare in the forest of Essex for the benefit of the sick or poor.

Fishermen living on the Essex coast often found their livelihoods at the mercy of the weather. For example, Essex suffered several great storms during the twelfth and thirteenth centuries, and from 1210 the Law of the Marsh required that people living near the coast should contribute to the upkeep of the sea defences. As with homes, wood was more plentiful than stone and so the sea walls were thatched with faggots and mended with wooden hurdles. By the end of the thirteenth century, supervision of these defences was in the hands of the king's justices and other officials appointed to temporary commissions on walls and ditches. The nuns of Barking recorded particularly high tides in the winter of 1376–77 and 'by the flooding of the Thames they have lost great part of the profit of their possessions at Berkying and elsewhere in Essex'.

The remains of star-shaped ponds dot the marshes today. These were the decoy ponds used for attracting wildfowl, and they were once a common feature of the Essex Marshes and many local families enjoyed duck for dinner.

Throughout the thirteenth century, London's growing population increased its demands for Essex produce. Southwest Essex, in particular, sent corn, wool and vegetables to London markets. Drovers bringing cattle from further north often used the Essex Marshes as a fattening ground, or at least a site for overwintering, before taking their livestock to market in London. Furthermore, Essex provided apprentices for the expanding trades in the capital.

HOMES AND VILLAGES: A MEDIEVAL LANDSCAPE
Most villages were small and often strung out along the sides of rivers or lanes. Farmhouses were often isolated, particularly towards the east coast. The open parklands of the larger manor houses dotted the landscape between the villages, and 900 medieval moated homes have been recorded in Essex.

The majority of medieval homes were based on a 'hall house': a single rectangular room, open to the roof timbers, with a central fireplace. Typical Essex houses were 12–16ft wide and two or more bays long. A 'bay' was the space between the upright timbers of the walls.

The principal building material in Essex was timber. Timber-framed walls were infilled with wattle and daub, and later often coated with lime wash plaster and a pink or white colourwash. In central and north Essex, decorative pargetting (raised plasterwork) was popular. In the south, weatherboarding was more common. Other important historic building materials include clay lump and pudding-stone in coastal areas, and clunch (a soft limestone) and flint from the north-west of Essex. Roofs were mostly thatched with some peg tile in the north and thatched or pantile (red fired-clay tile) roofs in the south of the county. By the early fifteenth century, those that could afford it built cross wings at the end of the hall, divided into two storeys with a parlour below and a solar upstairs.

Medieval Harwich grew rapidly and in 1318 it was given a charter, affording it similar privileges to those enjoyed by Colchester and Maldon.

THE SHERIFF OF ESSEX

Colchester remained the largest town in Essex throughout the Middle Ages. The castle acted as the county gaol and it is here that the Sheriff of Essex – the local representative of the king – would run the affairs of the county and preside over the courts.

Colchester Castle itself was outside the laws of both the parish and the borough. For example, men who were not 'freemen' could trade within the castle precinct and the borough officers could not arrest anyone there.

The Sokens too, Thorpe, Kirby and Walton, had enjoyed privileges of administering their own justice since Saxon times.

The list of medieval sheriffs includes many who left their mark on Essex. For example, Richard de Luci (Lucy), Sheriff from 1156–57, who built Ongar Castle; Simon de Pattishall (1193–94), remembered by a contemporary chronicler as one 'who guided the reins of the justices of the whole kingdom'; Hugh de Neville (1197–1200), the chief forester, in charge of all the royal forests; and Richard de Southchurch (1265–67), who bullied and cheated the Essex people out of goods and money for his own benefit. Several names, such as de Montfichet, Mancel, Delamar, Grapinel, Coggeshall and de la Lee, reappear on the list as sons, grandsons and great-grandsons succeeded to the same title. Until 1567, the Sheriff of Essex was also the Sheriff of Hertfordshire.

THE RISE OF CHELMSFORD

At the time of the *Domesday Book*, the manor on the site of the modern Chelmsford town centre was in the hands of the Bishop of London. It was less important than Moulsham, the larger manor south of the river, which Westminster Abbey owned. As the Roman bridge across the river had become unusable, people travelling between London and Colchester chose the road through Writtle, to avoid the Chelmsford river crossing.

However, about 1100, the Bishop of London, Maurice, built a new bridge across the Can. This provided a shorter, more convenient route on the Colchester road and Chelmsford began to see a rise in its fortunes. One hundred years later, another Bishop of London, William, obtained a market charter from the king and Chelmsford began to hold a weekly market near the bridge. Although Colchester was much larger than any other Essex town, from 1202 the royal justices regularly held the assizes trials at Chelmsford, and sometimes at Brentwood, since it was more central in Essex and nearer to London. By 1218, Chelmsford was recognised as the administrative centre for Essex. It took another 200 years, however, before buildings in Chelmsford stretched much beyond those lining the road between the bridge and the church.

COASTAL TRADE

Essex has a long coastline. It is also close to London. These facts helped the county's fortunes to rise, as dairy produce and meat could quickly be transported by sea for sale in London. Cereals and hay were also shipped to London along the Thames. Many small ports, hythes and quays developed during the Middle Ages in addition to those already used by fishermen. A survey of 1575 recorded 135 'Ports, Creeks and Landing places' in Essex, compared to twenty-nine in Suffolk and just eighteen in Kent.

In addition, there was direct trade from Thameside manors to the continent. For example, in 1367 John Burgeys of Fobbing obtained a royal warrant to ship sixty 'weys of cheese' to Flanders. Salt manufacturing was still providing a livelihood for several families and medieval salt-working sites have been identified on the north-east coast, for example at Marsh Farm, South Woodham Ferrers, Tollesbury Wick and at Morris Farm, Stow Maries.

THE ESSEX MARSHES, SHEEP AND SMUGGLERS

The Essex Marshes had not always been a benefit to the people who lived near them. You could not grow crops on them and they made it difficult – sometimes impossible – for boats to get into the shore. However, you could pasture sheep on the marsh. Essex became known for its huge, smelly sheep's milk cheeses. These were very popular with sailors as they would last for months on a long voyage. But more importantly, Essex became known for the quantity and quality of its wool.

From the late thirteenth century, English wool was being sold on the continent where it was in high demand from Flemish weavers. The best weavers lived in Belgium but the best wool came from England. In fact, wool became the backbone and driving force of the medieval English economy between the late thirteenth and late fifteenth centuries. Unfortunately for Essex labourers, however, it was those who owned huge flocks of sheep – like the monasteries – and the middlemen, the merchants who bought and sold the wool, who were making vast profits.

Edward I saw an opportunity to raise some extra money for the Crown and began to charge export duties on wool. This encouraged the 'owlers' – smugglers, who traded in wool to avoid the heavy taxes. Many an Essex village witnessed trains of pack horses loaded with bales of wool being led through the streets to the coast.

The sale and export of wool became more and more controlled, which made it harder for the small-scale shepherd on the Essex Marshes to share in the great wool wealth.

THE WOOL CHURCHES

Typical twelfth-century churches were built with slim lancet windows grouped into threes or fives, and their arches were pointed or trefoil, with deeply cut mouldings. Example architecture from this period can be seen in the churches at Wethersfield, Tilty, Easthorpe, Berden, Fairstead and Horndon-on-the-Hill.

Many churches benefited from huge investments by the nouveau-riche wool merchants. At St John's, Thaxted, for example, the church building was begun in 1340. Its growth continued for another 170 years, until it reached the dimensions of 183ft long and 87ft wide in 1510. The 80ft west tower of Thaxted church was added in the fifteenth century. The 181ft stone spire, the only medieval stone spire in Essex, was rebuilt three times when it was twice destroyed by lightning.

Besides wool, the people of Thaxted embraced the cutlery industry, approximately one-third of the adult men being involved in the industry during the fourteenth century. These crafts people included bladesmiths to make the

The Guildhall, Thaxted, built sometime between 1462–75 as a moote hall.

metal blades for the knives, swords or daggers. Handles would be made by a 'hafter', working with animal bone, while the 'sheather', made leather sheaths for the blades. A 'cutler' would combine all the parts into the finished product and would sell them. However, a lack of local sources of grinding stones contributed to the subsequent decline of the industry.

Thaxted Guildhall was built between 1462 and 1475 as a meeting place – a moote. The open, paved ground floor was used as a market, the first floor as a gallery for meetings, and the top floor was probably where the market warden lived. A charity took over the building in the late 1600s and it became a school providing education for thirty boys.

St Peter ad Vincula at Coggeshall is another example of a church which is much larger than necessary for the size of the village. Again, wealthy locals donated the funds to build its impressive structure.

FAIRS AND MARKETS

Throughout the Middle Ages, there were more and more applications for licences to hold fairs and local markets. In 1253 King Henry III granted Waltham Abbey the right to hold a weekly market as well as a three-day annual fair in May. These fairs and markets were strictly controlled to minimise competition. The market owner, usually the lord of the manor, made good profits from renting out stalls and collecting tolls.

The very name of Newport is Anglo-Saxon for 'new market'. It had a flourishing market for over 300 years from before the Conquest. However, Geoffrey de Mandeville, 1st Earl of Essex, moved the market to Walden. This new market was held inside the bailey of Geoffrey's castle, and for a while the town's name changed to reflect the importance of its market. It became Chipping Walden, meaning 'Market Walden'.

Romford had developed near the site of Roman Durolitum on the London to Colchester road. In 1247, Henry III (1216–72) granted Romford permission to hold a market every Wednesday, primarily as a sheep market and an outlet for the Hornchurch leather trade. As the Crown held the lordship, it was to Henry's financial benefit to allow the market.

Romford market was later one of only two licensed to provide supplies for the royal court in London. Sheep, cattle, pigs, geese and corn were sold from 1247 until 1958. The clerk of the market assigned free places in Romford market to townsmen, but charged others – butchers, glovers, smiths, shoemakers, and so on – to set up their stalls. At Halstead, Dunmow and Romford, householders fronting the market square were entitled to put up stalls under the eaves of their houses on market days and some of the innkeepers also profited by hiring out pens for animals, attached to hooks driven into the wooden studs of their buildings.

As the market started early, Londoners arrived on a Tuesday night to stay at the local inns. In 1579, Romford innkeeper John Bright left cash in his will so that his Tuesday guests, the London butchers, could have a memorial dinner in his honour

John Norden (1547–1625) notes that Chelmsford was known for its 'plentifull market of victuals corn and all necessaries'. Chelmsford market employed seven 'searchers' as well as a bailiff and clerk of the market. Their job was to check the quality of the goods offered for sale. Three of the searchers were for fish, victuals and meat, two for bread and ale, and two for leather.

So valuable were the rights to hold a fair that disputes often arose. The monks of St John's Abbey, Colchester, rowed with the townspeople about their Midsummer Fair in 1272. The abbot called a coroner to witness a dead body on St John's field. The man, said the monks, had been murdered by the townsmen. However, investigations found that the body was that of an executed criminal, taken from the town's gibbet and placed on the green by the monks themselves. Of course, relations were none the better after that. In 1290 the monks were ordered to pay 3s a year to the town: part of the money they were getting from the fair.

In 1285 the market days at Colchester were Wednesdays and Saturdays, but references in 1452 mention a daily market, possibly with different types of goods sold on different days. By 1825, the main market days were still Saturday (for corn and cattle) and Wednesday (for poultry and fruit). A pleasure fair held at Colchester at Eastertime included 'custard throwing'.

Much of the activity on market day centred on the moot halls or market crosses. These prominent buildings were for meetings or courts of law as well as for corn markets and other trading. Around them were the stalls for butchers and leather sellers. Ale tasters and bread weighers were often employed by the market officials to ensure fair trading. The stocks and pillory were near at hand. By the late 1700s, moot halls and market crosses had outlived their use and most of those in Essex were demolished; Steeple Bumpstead, Saffron Walden and Thaxted being notable exceptions.

SIR JOHN HAWKWOOD (c. 1320–94)

In 1337, Edward III embarked on the Hundred Years War. It was a golden opportunity for the son of an Essex yeoman with little excitement in his home town of Sible Hedingham, and so John Hawkwood joined the company of John de Vere of Castle Hedingham.

John proved himself a worthy soldier in the service of England. He obviously enjoyed the lifestyle as at the end of the war, he became a member of the White Company, a formidable band of mercenary soldiers numbering well into the hundreds. Eventually, John broke away from the main company to form his own group. They offered their services to the popes and rulers of the warring Italian states and became wealthy in the process. John's successes became renowned throughout Italy and he was well rewarded, not least by marriage to the daughter of Benardo Visconti of Milan. John Hawkwood is also remembered for his part in the shameful massacre at Cesna.

He died in Italy and was honoured with a memorial in El Duomo in Florence, alongside Italy's homegrown national heroes. His widow and son travelled to Sible Hedingham and settled there where John Hawkwood's Italian-designed effigy still adorns the town sign.

THOMAS WOODSTOCK, DUKE OF GLOUCESTER

Thomas Woodstock, the youngest child of Edward III, came to own Pleshey Castle when he married Eleanor de Bohun in 1376. He was knighted at the age of only 22 and later was awarded the title of the Duke of Gloucester.

However, Pleshey was not a happy place for poor Thomas. He was involved in the rebellion against Richard II in 1388. A few years later, Thomas agreed to meet with Richard at Pleshey but, unfortunately, it was the king's men who arrived. They captured Thomas and dragged him off to Calais where he was murdered. This incident features in Shakespeare's play, *Richard II*.

THE BLACK DEATH 1348–50

Like the rest of the country, Essex fared badly during the height of the Black Death. The disease spread across England, reaching Essex in the spring of 1349. Its effects were swiftly felt. In tiny Blackmore, for example, fifty-five people died between March and June 1349. North and central Essex lost nearly half its population, while Colchester itself lost only slightly fewer.

Distant relatives found themselves heirs to property while other cottages stood empty, depriving landlords of their rents. The shortage of labourers should have put the working classes in a strong position, able to demand higher wages, but the king brought in the Statue of Labourers in 1351, which fixed wages at their pre-plague levels.

THE PEASANTS' REVOLT

Labourers comprised nearly half the working population in the 1381 poll tax returns. Estimates suggest that only about 20 per cent of the adult population could read and write in agricultural counties like Essex.

Essex was at the forefront of the 1381 Peasants' Revolt. In fact, it all began when men from Fobbing, Corringham and Stanford-le-Hope were summoned to Brentwood to explain why they had not paid their taxes. The men became so angry that they attacked the tax man, John Bampton (also called Thomas), and the officials with him. These men escaped from the mob and reported back to their superiors.

Another group of commissioners, led by Chief Justice of the Common Pleas, Robert Belknap, arrived in Brentwood on 2 June 1381, but met with similar treatment. Their papers were seized and destroyed and a full-scale riot broke out. The Essex men grabbed three officials, sliced off their heads and did the same to three local jurors. Belknap escaped with his life but not his dignity. The murders prompted an outbreak of riot and plunder, which quickly spread across Essex.

The men of Kent were similarly furious at the situation. They communicated with Essex and soon a large group of men from both counties marched to London. The rabble was led by Wat Tyler, who lived in Kent but is thought to have had strong links with Essex. During the march, the rabble attacked large houses, ransacked churches and destroyed the paperwork that recorded tenancies and taxes. Court rolls, leases and charters were burnt in great bonfires at Chelmsford and Braintree.

The Coggeshall home of John Sewall, the sheriff, was ransacked, and John Ewell (Escheator of the County) was murdered at Langdon Hills. At Cressing Temple, the rebels destroyed the house of the king's treasurer, Sir Robert Hales. Angry labourers devastated Admiral Edmund de la Mare's manor at Peldon, while every document at Waltham Abbey was thrown onto a fire.

Colchester was taken over by a rampaging mob, some of whom turned their rage on foreign immigrants and killed several Flemish merchants. Other Flemings were killed at Manningtree.

In London, the 14-year-old Richard II rode out to meet the rebels at Mile End. He promised he would listen to their requests if they went home. The next day, 15 June, he met the rebels at Smithfield and Wat Tyler was struck dead by a soldier. Soon afterwards, John Ball, 'sometime priest of York and now of Colchester' who had supported the riots, was captured and executed at St Albans. John Starlyng, an Essex labourer, was accused of murdering Archbishop Simon Sudbury and was also hanged.

On 23 June, King Richard went into Waltham where he took back the promises he had made. Groups of rebels prepared themselves for confrontations at Billericay, Rettendon and Great Baddow. In fact, only the battle at Billericay took place. The rebels were no match for Richard's well-armed military and, when all hope was lost, the rebels abandoned the fight. Some hid in Norsey Wood near Wickford but were soon found and hanged by the king's men – it is said as many as 500 of them. The remaining peasants fled to Colchester or north into Suffolk

King Richard then rode into Chelmsford and again announced that there would be no extra rights or freedoms for peasants, revoking all the promises he had made a few weeks earlier. From 1–6 July 1381, Richard stayed at

Chelmsford, probably lodging at his manor house at Writtle and keeping a watchful eye on his unruly subjects. Some of the rebel leaders approached him to ask for pardon, but many of the ringleaders of the revolt were executed on the gallows at what is now Primrose Hill, Chelmsford.

RELIGIOUS NONCONFORMITY

An estimated 5,000–6,000 people lived in Colchester by 1400. It was at least five times larger than any other Essex town, although not particularly populous compared with towns in the rest of England.

The period immediately after the Black Death and the Peasants' Revolt was one of change and uncertainty. The authorities uncovered several groups of Lollards near Thaxted and Colchester. These religious groups who favoured preaching over traditional church services were acting outside of the law – a dangerous thing to do.

In November 1428, William Cheveling, a tailor, was burnt at the stake at Colchester's Balkerne Gate for heresy. Similarly, a 'prest of Thaksted' was burnt at the stake at Smithfield in 1431 for heresy. This may have been 'William' who is named in court records as being on trial for preaching in English (rather than the accepted Latin) to crowds in Maldon and Thaxted.

SPINNERS, WEAVERS AND CLOTHIERS

As early as 1304, clothmakers from Bruges in Belgium arrived at Harwich. They settled at Bocking and Shalford and established clothmaking businesses there. In fact, the majority of immigrants to Essex at this time were Flemish weavers and merchants.

Colchester was already making its own style of cloth – a medium quality grey or brown 'russet', 12 yards long and 2 yards wide. Later, weavers from Holland settled in Colchester too, helping Essex's clothmaking to become as successful as its production of raw wool.

By 1330, the woollen clothmaking business of mid- and north Essex employed a huge percentage of the population, including children as young as 6. It involved several distinct processes, each requiring a skilled craftsman. The spinning and carding of raw wool was performed by women; weavers then brought the spun yarn to weave; the fullers cleaned it (usually by soaking it in urine); the shearmen finished it, and the drapers sold the resultant cloth. Much of the cloth was exported from local quays, which increased employment and activity around the Essex coast.

In Colchester, the trade was regulated by the guilds, and workers concentrated into specific areas of town. They complained that their prosperity was challenged by the rural outworker system where village craftsmen and women worked at home in their own cottages.

In Coggeshall, markets expanded and opportunities grew for middlemen to co-ordinate the separate processes. These men, the clothiers, bought wool in bulk and delivered it to each of the craftsmen in turn, paying a wage for their labour, rather than a price for the finished product. Clothiers' servants led their laden packhorses through the streets, delivering supplies to each worker's cottage in turn. Thus, clothiers grew in wealth and importance while the rural craftsmen gradually lost their independence.

Butcher John Paycocke settled in Coggeshall around 1450. He prospered to such an extent that he was able to build a grand new house in West Street for his third son, Thomas, who had his own business as a clothier. By the time Thomas died in 1518, he was wealthy enough to leave bequests to several members of his family, friends, his apprentice, his weaver, his fuller and 12*d* apiece to 'all my weavers, fullers and shermen', and £4 to be divided among 'my kembers [combers], carders and spynners'.

Furthermore, he left £4 to Coggeshall Church and another
£4 to Coggeshall Abbey.

How surprised he would have been to find that within
twenty-five years of his death, the abbey would be dissolved
and its church demolished, while his own house would
stand practically unchanged for at least another 500 years.
Thomas' grand house, with pargetting and wooden carv-
ings inside and out displaying the family's ermine tail
symbol, demonstrates the rise of the middle classes, bridg-
ing the enormous gulf between rich and poor.

In 1538, the Essex weavers petitioned the courts that
they were being rendered destitute by rich clothiers who
colluded and 'agreed among themselves to hold and pay one
price for weaving', so that weavers could no longer support
their families. In 1555, the village weavers again complained that the 'wealthy Clothiers do many ways oppress
them'. The tables then turned in Colchester's favour again,
as the craftsmen's guilds protected their livelihoods against
the merchants.

BRIGHTLINGSEA: THE CINQUE PORT LIBERTY

The Cinque Ports were five named ports on the English
Channel. The system began before the Norman Conquest,
but its heyday was in the fourteenth and fifteenth centuries.
These towns had obligations to provide ships and men for
the king in time of war but, in return, were exempted from
some taxes. The ports were allowed to adopt 'limbs', which
were subsidiary ports to share in both the responsibilities
and benefits.

Brightlingsea became a limb of the port of Sandwich in
Kent, no doubt helping to fill the quota of ships requested
by the king. It was convenient for the Sandwichmen as a
halfway point to their annual herring fair at Yarmouth.
Furthermore, the Lord Warden, the head of the Cinque

Ports, had his own official oyster layings in Brightlingsea Creek until at least the 1670s.

On the negative side of the arrangement, much of the day-to-day administration of Brightlingsea was done in Kent. Sandwich magistrates had jurisdiction over Brightlingsea's taxes, petty criminals, licensing of inns and poor relief issues. Officials had to face a two-day journey by road or six hours by sea until an Act of Parliament in 1811 made Brightlingsea part of the Tendring hundred for local government and militia purposes.

Even today, on the first Monday in December, the freemen of Brightlingsea gather to elect the 'deputy of Brightlingsea', who becomes the representative of the Mayor of Sandwich.

HAVERING-ATTE-BOWER

The name Havering means 'the settlement of Haefer's people'. There is evidence of an estate at Havering belonging to Edward the Confessor, which was taken over by William I.

Havering Liberty, also called Havering-atte-Bower, was formed in 1465 and the suffix 'atte-Bower', meaning 'at the royal residence', was added to the name. A 'liberty' was an area where the king did not claim his usual rights. The lord of the manor had complete jurisdiction in the area and the townspeople benefited from certain rights (such as reduced taxes and being tried by their own local magistrates) similar to those of people living in the boroughs of Maldon (from 1171), Colchester (from 1189) and Harwich (from 1318).

Havering Park provided the Tudors with forty-three deer and three and a half oak trees each year. A series of boundary stones was set up in 1642 to mark the boundary of the liberty and the edge of Hainault Forest.

4

TUDOR ESSEX: WHERE HAVE ALL OUR MONASTERIES GONE?

The Tudor period was one of great upheaval for rich and poor alike, thanks to the strong personalities of the monarchs. Essex felt the disruptions more than most as the monarchs took a personal interest in the county: its hunting forests, its growing wealth from wool and trade, its luxurious grand houses and its interesting, well-connected people.

GREAT TUDOR PERSONALITIES

The Tudor monarchs surrounded themselves with advisors, rewarding them handsomely to ensure their loyalty. Many of these were Essex men, who became highly influential in the history of Britain:

> John de Vere (*c.* 1482–1540) the 15th Earl of Oxford, of Castle Hedingham, was Lord Great Chamberlain and a Knight of the Garter. He carried the crown at Anne Boleyn's coronation.

Thomas Audley (*c.* 1488–1544), from Earls Colne, became Speaker of the House of Commons (1529–33), Lord Keeper of the Great Seal (1532) and Lord Chancellor (1533–44).

Sir William Petre (*c.* 1505–72) was born in Devon but acquired Ingatestone Hall during the Dissolution and founded a great Essex dynasty. He was Secretary of State to four successive Tudor monarchs: Henry VIII, Edward VI, Mary I and Elizabeth I, despite his Catholic sympathies.

Thomas Darcy of St Osyth (1506–58) was created Baron Darcy of Chiche in 1551 and became Lord Chamberlain of the Household.

Sir Walter Mildmay (*c.* 1523–89) of Moulsham served as Chancellor of the Exchequer under Elizabeth I.

Sir Thomas Smith (1513–77) was born in Saffron Walden, but is known for his magnificent estate at Hill Hall near Epping. He was Secretary of State to both Edward VI and Elizabeth I, and Chancellor of the Order of the Garter.

KING HENRY VIII (REIGNED 1509–47)

Henry VIII was fond of Essex, and certainly very familiar with it. Even before he became king, he lived at Wanstead Hall, then a royal hunting lodge. Wanstead remained a royal manor for some years, its 'keeper' being an office awarded to favoured royal courtiers.

In 1517 Henry bought New Hall from Thomas Boleyn, changed the building's name to Beaulieu, and enlarged it into a palace. On 23 July 1527, Henry's court arrived at Beaulieu on his summer progress, staying, unusually, for over a month in the company of a large number of nobles and their wives. For many years, Mary Tudor lived at New Hall waiting for other people to decide her fate. The estate was later bought by Oliver Cromwell.

Henry was also a frequent visitor to Blackmore where the priory was known as Jericho. Here, he had private meetings with his mistress, Elizabeth Blount, the mother of his only acknowledged illegitimate child, Henry Fitzroy, who was born there.

In 1541, Henry acquired Pyrgo in Havering. It was here that the king had a rare meeting with his daughters: Mary, then 23, and Elizabeth, just 8 years old. Following the encounter, he formally acknowledged his daughters' right of succession to the throne, which allowed them to rule after their brother, Edward VI. (The original house at Pyrgo was eventually replaced with a more modest Victorian gentleman's residence, which Essex County Council purchased and then demolished in 1937 as part of the Metropolitan Greenbelt scheme.)

Waltham Abbey passed ownership of Copped Hall to Henry VIII, possibly as a bribe to prevent him from dissolving the abbey. However, Henry just said, 'thank you very much', and closed the abbey anyway. In 1548 Edward VI allowed his half-sister Mary to live at Copped Hall, although she remained a prisoner. When Mary became queen in 1533, Copped Hall was leased to Sir Thomas Cornwallis. In 1558, it was transferred to the Duchy of Lancaster. In 1564, Queen Elizabeth granted the hall to one of her closest friends, Sir Thomas Heneage. He improved the mansion so much that Elizabeth stayed there on one of her progresses through the county.

The forests of Essex continued to provide rich hunting grounds for the gentry – a favourite sport of Henry's – and provided timber for building projects. Westminster Abbey and St Paul's Cathedral owned significant tracts of woodland in Essex which they sold as coppice or used in their own construction projects. Timber from Hadleigh Great Wood may have been used in the rebuilding of St Paul's Cathedral after the Great Fire of London.

When Henry VIII's growing navy demanded ships of ever-increasing capacity, Essex forests again provided the timber to the shipbuilding ports of Barking, Leigh, Maldon and Harwich. In 1519 Henry hired eleven carpenters to hew thirty-one loads of timber from Thundersley Park towards the building of his ship the *Kateryn Pleasunce*. Similarly, the *Merchant Royal* (later destroyed by the Spanish Armada) was built for Elizabeth I in 1574 with timber grown in Essex.

Successive monarchs issued frequent orders to the Sheriff of Essex to see that the bridges in his county were in a good state, chiefly to ensure that royal hunting expeditions were not delayed. However, many bridges remained unrepaired as it was difficult to discover who was responsible for paying the carpenter. An Act of Parliament in 1531 allocated responsibility for bridge repair to the county Justices of the Peace, with the right to levy a county rate to pay for the cost. This ensured that bridges along main routes were repaired at county expense, such as Moulsham Bridge across the Can at Chelmsford.

THE DISSOLUTION

In the years between William's Conquest and Henry VIII's notorious Dissolution of the Monasteries, at least forty-seven religious houses had been established in Essex, consisting of:

Two mitred abbeys – Waltham Holy Cross and St John's Colchester.

Six common abbeys – Beeleigh, Coggeshall, St Osyth, Stratford-Longthorn, Tilty and Walden.

Twenty-two priories – Burden, Blackmore, St Botolph, Bicknacre, Maldon, Chelmsford, Dunmow, Grey Friars at Colchester, Earls Colne, Hatfield Broad Oak, Hatfield Peverell, Little Horkesley, Latton, Little Lees, West Mersea, Panfield, Prittlewell, Stansgate, Takeley, Tiptree, Thoby and Thremhall.

Three nunneries – Barking, Hedingham and Wix.

Three colleges – Halstead, Pleshey and Layer Marney.

Two preceptories of Templars – Cressing and Little Maplestead.

Nine hospitals – Bocking; a leper hospital at Brook Street in South Weald; Castle Hedingham; Hornchurch; Great Ilford; Newport; St. Giles' at Maldon; Crouched Friars at Colchester and St Mary Magdalen at Colchester.

Beeleigh Abbey, founded in 1180 for the Premonstratensian canons and dissolved in 1536.

However, religious houses had been declining for many years before the Dissolution. Five in Essex had 'long been closed' by the time Henry VIII's auditors enquired into them. Bicknacre Priory died out 'through poverty' by 1507 and Latton Priory was deserted by 1534. Cardinal Wolsey had already dissolved thirty English monasteries between 1524 and 1527, claiming that they were corrupt. He also shut down six priories (for example, Little Horkesley and Blackmore) and used their wealth towards building his colleges at Ipswich and Christ Church at Oxford.

Henry VIII himself was convinced that he could never be free of the Pope while the monasteries existed. In 1536, Henry closed all religious houses that had an income of less than £200 a year. The seven remaining houses in Essex had all surrendered to him by 1540. There were few protests. The monks went quietly and some were offered positions as local clergy, while others received a pension, only the youngest were cast out with no compensation. Only the

Abbot of St John's, Colchester, resisted. He said, 'The king shall never have my house but against my will and against my heart.' He was tried for treason and his head was chopped off.

Occasionally, a parish bought part of a monastic church for its own use. This happened at Little Dunmow, Tilty and Little Horkesley. At Waltham Abbey too, the churchwardens pleaded for the monastery nave to become the parish church as it has been used by the townspeople 'from time immemorial'. Here at Waltham, the Dissolution dismayed the whole town as many townspeople had earned their living from the abbey and the pilgrims it attracted.

At Hatfield Broad Oak, the rest of the monastic buildings became a private residence. In most cases, however, the king's agents stripped the monasteries of their contents and roofing and allowed them to fall into ruin. Stone was used in the king's own building projects – for example, stone from Barking Abbey was shipped across the Thames to help construct Henry's new manor house at Dartford, and lead from the roof was used to repair the roof of Greenwich Palace. To the King's Jewel House went 3,586 ounces of gilt silver plate from Barking Abbey, plus a beryl-decorated silver gilt monstrance weighing 65 ounces. Cattle and other livestock were sold for £182 2*s* 10*d*.

The king then sold the lands belonging to the monastic estates. This amounted to about two-fifths of the area of Essex, and was the biggest change in land ownership since 1066. Thomas Audley received the former Walden Priory and converted it into a private residence. His son-in-law, Thomas Howard, 4th Duke of Norfolk, inherited the property and extended it into a grand Elizabethan mansion. He renamed the property Audley End. The magnificent house – even grander than what remains of it today – bankrupted the family.

A few years after the monasteries closed, the chantries and religious guilds, some fifty in Essex, were also dissolved. Their monetary value was small but it was a great loss to the religious life of the people of Essex. Education also suffered – or was at least disrupted – because almost every Essex chantry priest had acted as a schoolmaster or as a curate to his parish.

However, Henry had his eye on individuals as well as the religious organisations and although his persecution never reached the heights of that of his daughters, he arrested forty people for heresy at Colchester, Braintree and Witham as early as 1527, and another eighty people at Steeple Bumpstead soon afterwards.

RICHARD LORD RICH (1496/7-1567)

Sir Richard Rich, Lord Rich of Leighs, benefited enormously from the Dissolution, acquiring forty-three manors in Essex during the reign of Henry VIII, including his main residence: Leighs (Leez) Priory. Here, Rich demolished many of the priory buildings and replaced them with a magnificent brick mansion. The priory church was incorporated into his new house and he kept the monastic fish ponds.

By the end of the Tudor period, Rich owned sixty-four Essex manors (and he had sold another twelve), obtained by purchase at reduced prices or as gifts from the monarch. Throughout his life he shifted his political and religious allegiances to further his career, and his double-dealing and self-serving actions are now notorious.

Rich had trained as a lawyer and became MP for Colchester in 1529, partly due to support from Thomas Audley and John de Vere. He was knighted in 1533 and became Solicitor General and later, Speaker of the House of Commons. During the reign of Edward VI, Rich was Lord Chancellor (1547–52).

He played a significant role in the downfall of Thomas More, Thomas Cromwell (both former 'friends' of his) and Bishop John Fisher, as well as many ordinary citizens who

The seal of St Osyth's Priory.

burned at the stake for their religious beliefs. Furthermore, during Mary's reign, he personally turned the handle on the Tower of London rack that tortured a young Protestant woman, Anne Askew. Despite this, Rich employed a private Protestant priest for his family chapel and appointed Protestant or even Puritanical vicars to churches under his control.

In 1564 Rich established the Free School of Richard Lord Rich (now the Felsted School) near his Leez estate – ironically, its motto is 'Keep Your Faith'. Perhaps mindful of his own soul and with the idea of fooling God in the same way as he had played the monarchs, Rich bequeathed money for almshouses to be built in Felsted and in Rochford.

Despite these tiny generosities and his magnificent effigy in Felsted Church, this ruthless and duplicitous man was named by *BBC History Magazine* as the wickedest villain of the sixteenth century.

THOMAS MILDMAY (c. 1515–66) AND WALTER MILDMAY (c. 1520–89)

Two other 'winners' during the Dissolution were ambitious Chelmsford brothers, Thomas and Walter Mildmay. Their father, also Thomas Mildmay, had owned a stall at Chelmsford Market with enough success to enable him to buy 'Guy Harlings', a grand house in the town, in 1527 (now Chelmsford Cathedral diocesan office).

Thomas Jnr trained in accountancy and obtained a position as an auditor assisting with the process of the monastery dissolutions. He may have been working directly under Richard Rich, and was involved in the dissolution of the lesser religious houses in East Anglia throughout 1536 and 1537.

Thomas spent some of his earnings on a former monastic property in Chelmsford valued at nearly £80. In 1540, he then bought the whole manor of Moulsham for about £620. Here, he lavishly rebuilt Moulsham Hall hoping to turn it into 'the greatest esquire's building within the county of Essex'.

Thomas worked his way up to be the most important auditor in the government. He did much work in the Duchy of Cornwall and became MP for Cornwall at least six times. Through him, his brother Walter also became an administrator and accountant for the king. He sat as an MP for Cornwall, and later for Maldon. He too invested in property, purchasing Fingrith Hall in Blackmore and Seynclers and Herons in Danbury. For his main country house, however, he purchased the magnificent Apethorpe Hall in Northamptonshire.

Having Puritan sympathies, the brothers kept a low profile during Mary's reign but flourished again under Elizabeth I. During Elizabeth's reign, Thomas became Sheriff of Essex. He remained active in public affairs until his death in 1566. Walter, meanwhile, became a privy councillor and from 1566 to his death in 1589, was Elizabeth's Chancellor of the Exchequer.

Not bad for two lads from Chelmsford Grammar School.

LAYER MARNEY TOWER

Layer Marney Tower is, at 80ft, England's tallest Tudor gatehouse, and was built in the 1520s during the reign of Henry VIII. Henry Lord Marney envisaged it as an ostentatious gateway to an even more magnificent palace. However, the tower was completed but the palace was not. Unfortunately for Lord Marney, he died just three years after he began his lavish project. His son, John, planned to execute his father's vision but he too died, just two years after his father.

Lord Marney was Lord Privy Seal of Henry's court, and Captain of the Bodyguard. Like other courtiers, he wanted his home to reflect his status. Although the crenellations were to be purely decorative, rather than fortifications, King Henry still had to give his permission for them to be used on the tower. The red bricks

Layer Marney Towers, the tallest Tudor gatehouse in England, built by Henry Lord Marney in the 1520s.

were chosen to mimic expensive imported stone and the windows placed to make the tower appear to have more floors than it actually had. However, the black-glazed bricks that make a decorative diapering pattern on the tower, did come from Italy. There are ninety-nine steps in each tower.

Sir Brian Tuke, Treasurer to the Royal Household and Governor of the King's Posts, bought the tower and his son, George, entertained Elizabeth I there for two days in 1561.

KING EDWARD VI (REIGNED 1547–53)

Edward VI oversaw the continued destruction of Catholic icons and artefacts in churches throughout England. Beautiful paintings were whitewashed over, statues smashed and chalices confiscated. At Great Dunmow, the churchwardens recorded that their stone altar was broken up and replaced with a wooden communion table. The carved rood screen was pulled down and destroyed. Furthermore, the king's officials brought in a new book with the service in English, not Latin.

The king's officials toured the county inspecting the churches and reported back when the paintings had not been covered or the stained glass removed from the windows. In many instances, the church plate and vestments could not be found when the inspectors called. Some were miraculously returned when Mary became queen; others were never seen again.

At Leigh, the stained-glass depictions of the coats of arms of previous lords of the manor were removed from the church. Later, this valuable glass could not be found to be reinstated. Years later, it was rediscovered – adorning the back windows of the house where the churchwarden had been living at the time.

Lord Rich obtained ten more manors during Edward's reign, including his second favourite home, Rochford Hall (formerly Mary Boleyn's home), and the former hunting lodge at Wanstead. This latter he replaced with Wanstead House, a fine country seat, reportedly the largest in Essex at the time. The building boasts an impressive list of owners: Robert Dudley, Earl of Leicester; Charles Blount, Earl of

Devonshire; George Villiers, Duke of Buckingham; and Sir
Henry Mildmay.

EARLY EDUCATION

The oldest still existing school in Essex is the Colchester
Royal Grammar School which was founded in 1206.
Most early schools were attached to monasteries so, at the
Dissolution, schools and teachers disappeared as well as the
religious houses. The grammar schools taught Latin grammar, which was a requirement for boys who wanted to go
up to university.

Henry VIII supported education in order to provide the
next generation of leaders and therefore re-founded many
schools. Colchester Grammar School, for example, was
granted a royal charter by Henry VIII to enable it to continue. Elizabeth I granted a second charter to the school,
which confirmed the school's right to exist and to be run by
the parish clergy, rather than monks.

As part of the efforts to control religious beliefs, chantry
schools were closed down. These were schools attached to
a church with a schoolmaster (often the curate) paid for by
a private benefactor. Some of these had not been in existence for long. For example, Maldon Grammar School
was founded in 1407 to instruct the sons of fishermen. A
chantry school was also founded at Chesterford in 1514,
and another at Earls Colne in 1518.

Chantry schools were sometimes held in the church
porch (as at Thaxted) and concentrated on moral and religious education. A school at Finchingfield had thirty pupils
taught by a priest of a Trinity Guild, a semi-religious society
set up by local people and, therefore, outside the control of
the established church. At Hornchurch, school was taught
by the priest of another Trinity Guild, who was paid £5 4s
11d a year. At Great Chesterford, the priest in charge of

the twenty scholars was paid out of the rents received from land donated by William Holden.

In Saffron Walden, John Leche built the schoolhouse and gave lands to the Trinity Guild in 1517 to provide £10 a year to find a priest who 'shall be a profound gramarion to the intent that he may teche grammar within the towne'. In fact, Saffron Walden boys had had access to schooling for many years. Two chaplains had been called before the abbot of Walden Abbey in 1423 to explain why they had been 'teaching small boys of Walden and instructing them in the alphabet and graces' without permission from him. The 'graces' were the prayers recited before and after eating meat.

Most of the chantry schools were re-founded as 'free schools' by the end of Edward's reign. In addition to the continuation of these schools, several others were founded where none had existed before. Edward VI encouraged the establishment of free grammar schools for non-fee-paying pupils. It is Edward's re-founding of schools with new charters which has led to many being named for him. King Edward VI Grammar School in Chelmsford is a case in point.

At the suggestion of the Mildmay brothers, Edward VI issued a royal warrant to establish a free grammar school in March 1551 for the education of boys in Chelmsford and Moulsham in the Anglican religion and Classical languages (Latin and Greek). Initially, pupils were taught in part of an old friary in Moulsham. The Mildmays, Sir Henry Tyrrell and Sir William Petre were in charge of the endowments which funded the school, giving it land worth £22. Sadly, the endowment land had all been sold by 1957 when the governors made the decision to become a state, rather than an independent school. The Mildmay family were connected with the school for 327 years.

Maldon's Plume Grammar School was founded in 1608.

QUEEN JANE IN ESSEX

Lady Jane Grey (Queen of England for nine days in 1553) had many supporters in Essex. One such was Sir John Gates of Beeleigh Abbey, a former Sheriff of Essex. Unfortunately for him, he lost his head a year before Jane lost hers. For a while, Jane's younger sister, Catherine, was kept under house arrest at Pyrgo Place, Essex, by Elizabeth I.

QUEEN MARY I ('BLOODY MARY', REIGNED 1553–58)

Henry VIII's daughter, Mary, spent much of her early life at New Hall (Beaulieu) and at Copt (Copped) Hall in Essex until she became queen in 1553. A staunch Catholic, on becoming Queen Mary immediately insisted that the English Church accept the rule of the Pope. The Great Dunmow churchwardens tried to restore their church by bringing back banners for church processions and paying for the binding of a new Latin service book. They paid 'Father Andrews', an old carpenter, for making a cross of timber for a makeshift rood.

Mary was responsible for the deaths of sixty-three Essex people. Their crime was 'heresy' and they came from all walks of life. They included Hugh Laverstok, a lame painter from Barking; Thomas Higbed, a farmer from Horndon; Thomas Bowyer, a weaver from Great Dunmow; Mr Newman, a pewterer from Saffron Walden; George Ambrose, a fuller from Brocking; William Tyms, a curate of Hockley, and Thomas Causton, a gentleman of Thundersley and Tillingham. By contrast, twenty-one Catholics were hanged drawn and quartered (the women just hanged) for their faith during the Tudor period. Their crime was cited as 'treason'.

Lord Rich only acquired six additional manors during Mary's reign – still quite a feat considering his Puritan sympathies.

Saffron Walden obtained a borough charter in 1549, followed by Great Dunmow and Thaxted in 1556. These charters allowed the townspeople to raise money, for example by buying and then renting out land, and to administer their own taxes.

WILLIAM HUNTER

William Hunter was 19 when he lost his job as a London silk weaver and returned to his parents' home in Brentwood in 1555. He wandered into the chapel on Brentwood High Street one day and began to read the Bible there. The priest came in and challenged William.

William – whether he was brave or foolish is a matter of opinion – began to argue his religious beliefs and found himself taken before the local magistrate. William refused to agree with the Catholic teachings which were the accepted beliefs. Brought before Bishop Bonner in London, he resisted both bribes and threats. Bonner offered him the huge sum of £40 but William refused it.

Eventually, Bonner ordered William's execution. He was returned to Brentwood where he was burnt at the stake in front of the townspeople, including his family.

An elm tree was planted on the site of William's death.

THE COLCHESTER MARTYRS

Twenty-five people were burnt at the stake in Colchester for their religious beliefs between 1545 and 1558. Most of them were ordinary men and women: weavers, tanners and husbandmen. With all these heretics being found, it was convenient for the authorities to burn several at the same time on one huge fire.

In August 1557, ten men from Colchester were burnt at the stake by the Balkerne Gate. Not long afterwards, another ten were burnt, again all together in the same fire.

Although tried in London, they were returned to their local areas to be executed as a lesson to other people. The townspeople were deliberately called to come to watch the burning lest they be thought of as Protestant sympathisers. There is a memorial to the martyrs in Colchester Town Hall.

THE STRATFORD MARTYRS

A vast crowd gathered in Stratford when nine men and two women were driven through the town in an open cart and burnt together on 27 June 1556. They were a mixed bunch: Henry Adlington, a sawyer of Grinstead; Laurence Pernam, a smith from Hoddesdon; Henry Wye, a brewer from Stanford-le-Hope; William Halliwel, a smith from Waltham Holy Cross; Thomas Bowyer, a weaver from Great Dunmow; George Searles, a tailor, of White Notley; Edmund Hurst, a labourer from Colchester; Lyon Cawch, a Flemish merchant from the City of London; Ralph Jackson, a servant from Chipping Ongar; John Derifall, a labourer from Rettendon; John Routh, a labourer from Wix; Elizabeth Pepper of Colchester, who was pregnant, and Agnes George from West Bergholt.

When Bishop Bonner had failed to get any of them to recant their beliefs, he had ordered them to be taken to Stratford. Here, they were put into two separate rooms. An official came to each group and told them that the other group had recanted and had been released. However, whether they realised it was a trick or not, nobody actually altered their plea. Therefore, all eleven were brought out of the rooms to where an enormous fire had been built in the middle of the street. Hired labourers put the finishing touches to the pile of dry wood; the executioner waited quietly for the signal to light his torch and the officials stood by, eager to see justice done. And surrounding it all, hundreds of ordinary people from Stratford and across the neighbouring villages crowded around – some trying to sell their goods to the crowd, some keen to see the spectacle, others wishing it was not happening. Among the crowd were the relatives of the condemned people: their husbands, wives, children, parents and siblings.

The men were tied to three separate stakes, set up in the middle of the wood pile. The two women were pushed into the middle of them. Then the executioner set the flame to the pyre and the eleven died together in agony.

The exact location of the burning is not known. It may have been the Fair Field in Bow. A monument to the martyrs was erected in St John's churchyard, Stratford Broadway, in 1879.

QUEEN ELIZABETH I, 1558–1603

Elizabeth I, like her father, spent a lot of time in Essex. This was a favourite hunting ground as well as home to several of her favourite people.

In the 1580s, Elizabeth reintroduced the office of Lord Lieutenant of the County (the Duke of Northumberland had first created this office in the wake of the peasant rebellions of 1549). The Lord Lieutenant took over the sheriff's military duties in the county and was responsible for levying the militia. The Essex Militia was formed under Henry VIII and continued by Elizabeth. Her law was that all lower to middle-class men who owned land were to meet at least once a month to train in the art of warfare. They learnt how to use a pike and a longbow. This militia could be called out to defend England at a moment's notice, supported by as many untrained locals as were called.

Elizabeth was not as ruthless as her sister Mary. Nevertheless, her reign was a dangerous time to be a Catholic. For example, John Paine was tortured, hanged, drawn and quartered at Chelmsford in April 1582 for his Catholic beliefs. No other Catholics were martyred during Elizabeth's reign, possibly because Catholic sympathisers,

the Petre family, were such good hosts to Her Majesty at
Ingatestone Hall. (Ingatestone Hall does, however, contain a secret 'priest's hole', which suggests the Petre family
were not complacent about the queen's friendship.)

A QUEEN'S PROGRESS: ELIZABETH I IN ESSEX

It is easy to see which were the finest houses and the most
respected people in Essex during Elizabeth's reign from
examining the visits she made in the county. The queen's
progresses were famous. She not only took her clothing and
belongings, but also hundreds of members of her household. They travelled across the country to stay for a few
days at other people's houses, visiting Essex at least sixty-
seven times.

In July 1561, she was entertained by Lord Rich at
Wanstead before travelling on to Havering Palace and
Pyrgo (Lord John Grey) to Loughton Hall (John Stonard/
Stoner). She spent a night at Ingatestone Hall (Sir William
Petre), before staying at New Hall (Thomas Radclyffe,
3rd Earl of Sussex). After five days, she moved on to Felix
Hall at Kelvedon (Henry Long), then St John's at Colchester
(Sir Thomas Lucas), Layer Marney (George Tuke) and
St Osyth (Lord Darcy). She returned to Colchester on
1 August, then spent three days in Harwich, en route to
Suffolk. She returned from Suffolk to Castle Hedingham
(John de Vere, 16th Earl of Oxford). On 19 August she
travelled to Gosfield Hall (Sir John Wentworth), Leez Priory
(Richard Lord Rich) and Great Hallingbury (Lord Morley),
then into Hertfordshire before finally returning to London
in late September.

Church bells pealed as the queen arrived at each town
(the ringers being paid in beer as well as money), while the
townsfolk welcomed her with entertainments and gifts such
as a silver or gold cup. James Woodhall, the treasurer of
Saffron Walden, presented the queen with a silver double
gilt cup with cover valued at £19 3s when she stayed

at Audley End in 1571, and also helped to raise the £37 needed for her reception.

When Elizabeth left Harwich in 1561 she asked the townspeople what she could do for them. The reply was, 'Nothing but to wish your Majesty a good journey'. The queen replied that Harwich was 'a pretty Town and wants nothing'.

WILLIAM GILBERD

When Elizabeth was not travelling into Essex, she received many Essex-born people at her court. Not least among these was William Gilberd, who became her physician.

Gilberd, born in Colchester in 1544, not only practised medicine but also experimented with magnetism and static electricity, proving that two difference forces were at work. He experimented with a model of the globe and his work informed other scientists who went on to invent compasses and formally recognise electricity. Thus, William Gilberd is sometimes named 'the father of electricity'.

EDWARD DE VERE

Young Edward de Vere of Hedingham Castle was also a favourite of the queen. He had been a ward of court (in practice, living under the roof of William Cecil) since the age of 12, when his father died. Edward, the 17th Earl of Oxford, counted Queen Elizabeth among the guests at his wedding to Anne Cecil in 1571, but he later displeased the queen when he had an affair with a maid of honour.

Edward enjoyed the theatre and writing poetry. He has many supporters for the idea that he wrote plays under the pseudonym 'William Shakespeare'. Certainly, he had associations with some of the personalities in Shakespeare's plays and he travelled to several Shakespearean locations in Europe. Edward died in London of plague in 1604, aged 54.

TILBURY FORT

Henry VIII chose Tilbury as a location for two block-houses as part of London's defences against the French, the Spanish and everyone else he had upset. The East Tilbury blockhouse was on the riverbank at Coalhouse Point about half a mile south of the present village. It crossed its fire with the Higham blockhouse on the Kent shore to form the first line of defence in the river, the second line being the Tilbury, Gravesend and Milton blockhouses, 3 miles upstream. It cost £506 to build each blockhouse, even though they recycled materials from the dissolved St Margaret's Chapel nearby.

Tilbury Fort's Watergate, commissioned by Charles II in 1670 when the fort's defences were upgraded.

When the Spanish invasion seemed even more likely in the 1580s, Elizabeth I commissioned Italian engineer Frederico Genebelli to upgrade the blockhouse at West Tilbury with star-shaped earthworks. It was here that Elizabeth came when a Spanish invasion seemed likely. Officials, soldiers and local people gathered to see the queen sitting on a white charger, and hear her give her famous rousing speech (although how many of the hundreds present actually heard her speak the words is debatable):

> Let tyrants fear ... I am come amongst you ... to live or die amongst you all, to lay down my life for my God and for my kingdom and for my people, my honour, and my blood, even in the dust.

In 1670, new life was given to the project of building a fort at Tilbury when Charles II approved a new design for a pentagonal fort with five bastions. The Watergate was to be the fort's main entrance and impressive facade, as most supplies and visitors would arrive by river. However, the fort did not see military action until the First World War when its anti-aircraft guns shot down a Zeppelin. In the Second World War, a bomb destroyed the barracks on the west of the parade ground.

WHICH WITCH? ELIZABETH BENNET AND URSULA KEMP

In 1563, Elizabeth I updated her father's law against witchcraft, and the first person prosecuted and hanged under this new Act was Elizabeth Lowys from Great Waltham.

The first witch trials in a secular court in England were at Chelmsford in 1566, where the trial of three women resulted in the hanging of Agnes Waterhouse. In fact, Chelmsford holds the record for hanging more women for witchcraft than any other town in England. The statistics from court records are indeed food for thought – between 1560 and 1700, seventeen people were formally accused of witchcraft in Sussex, fifty-two in Hertfordshire, ninety-one in Kent, and 299 in Essex.

Times were hard in 1582. Grace Thurlow refused to employ Ursula Kemp to look after her new daughter, shortly after which the baby fell from its cot and died. Ursula was reported to the local magistrate, Brian Darcy of St Clere's Hall, St Osyth. Brian was the youngest of three sons and was keen to make a name for himself. The previous year he had been embarrassed when ordered to release a 13-year-old boy who he had imprisoned on charges of being a magician's apprentice. He was determined, this time, to secure a conviction.

Ursula was taken from her humble home to a hastily convened court at St Clere's Hall. She denied the accusations. Brian then invited the woman to walk with him in his garden. When they returned to the court, Ursula not only confessed to all the charges but also named three other 'witches' in the area.

News of the case spread quickly and, seeing an opportunity to be rid of their own local witches, women were brought from Little Clacton, Little Oakley, Thorpe le Soken and Walton-on-the-Naze. Most of those questioned confessed and implicated others, too. Within five weeks, thirteen people – twelve women and one man (a traditional witches' coven) – had been questioned by the court.

Brian Darcy was confident enough of his prisoners' guilt (hadn't he heard their confessions from their own mouths?) that he committed them to Colchester Gaol to await trial at the assizes (a superior court necessary for trying serious felonies). In the end, nine of the accused were sent to the next Chelmsford Assizes. Five of the nine were found guilty of murder. Three of those were sentenced to imprisonment and two to death by hanging. Imprisonment was no soft option: the airless, unsanitary, fetid room in the basement of Colchester Castle was often a death sentence itself.

Ursula Kemp and Elizabeth Bennet were immediately taken from the court room and were hanged, probably at Primrose Hill, to the entertainment of the people of Chelmsford. The two bodies were dipped in pitch and displayed in Chelmsford High Street for a few days before being returned to St Osyth's. Iron rivets were driven through the ankles, knees and wrists of the bodies before they were consigned to a patch of unconsecrated ground.

However, that is not the end of the story. In 1921, the grave of the two women was accidentally uncovered, the rivets still in situ in their bones. The skeletons were put on display, later sold to a museum, and eventually in 2011 reburied in a secret plot in St Osyth's.

A Dutch cottage, Canvey Island, built by Dutch immigrants in 1618.

MOSQUITOS ON THE MARSHES

Sheep farmers were having a new difficulty of their own from the mid-1500s. About this time, mosquitos were unwittingly imported to England, probably as stowaways on trading ships. They found an ideal breeding ground in the coastal marshes and thrived. Unfortunately, the mosquitos carried a deadly ague (the malaria virus).

John Norden wrote in 1594, 'I can not comende the helthfulnes of it [Essex]: And especiallie nere the sea coastes, Rochford, Denge, Tendring hundreds and other lowe places about the creekes, which gave me a most cruell quarterne fever'. The ague was not generally fatal to those born and bred on the coast, but could be so to those that came in from outside. It is not mentioned prior to the sixteenth century and its advent may have been linked to increased trade with the Orient and Africa.

In 1722, Daniel Defoe recorded that men who took wives who were not local to the coast soon became widowers and had to find new wives. The poor girls coming from inland Essex had no immunity and often died of ague. The disease declined rapidly in the nineteenth century for a variety of reasons, including the introduction of quinine and the increased drainage of the marshes.

5

STUART ESSEX:
A CIVIL WAR

By 1600, more than 300 houses existed in Chelmsford plus many inns. The buildings were of 'timber and tile', and over the previous fifty years several had had upper storeys added. Saffron Walden was at least equal in size to Chelmsford, with as many as 375 buildings, seven inns and five mills which attracted London merchants.

Meanwhile, John Norden tells us that Harwich, in 1600, was 'little, well compacte and thenste [narrow]'. William Camden, writing in 1590, thought, 'Harwich is a town of hurry and business, not much of gaiety and pleasure'. He went on to say that Brentwood, Ingatestone and even Chelmsford:

> ... have very little to be said of them, but that they are large thoroughfare towns, full of good inns, and chiefly maintained by the excessive multitude of carriers and passengers, which are constantly passing this way to London with droves of cattle, provisions and manufactures for London.

A survey in 1634 suggested that half the working population of Essex was engaged in the cloth industry or related occupations. However, in much of the county, agriculture still dominated, with the chalky boulder clay soils of north and north-western Essex being ideal for growing wheat and barley. The London clay of the south was more suited to dairy farming and, of course, sheep still grazed the marshes.

Essex natives spoke the country dialect associated with East Anglian agricultural communities. Londoners were 'furriners'.

DUTCH AND FRENCH WEAVERS IN COLCHESTER

In 1562 over 1,000 Huguenots were massacred in France. Their friends and relatives fled to England, many settling in Essex. Similarly, exiled weavers coming from the Netherlands found their way to Colchester from 1565 and settled in such numbers to establish a 'Dutch quarter' of the town.

In the 1570s, another influx of Flemish refugees escaping Spanish persecution reinvigorated the East Anglian weaving trade, which appeared to be in decline. They settled particularly in Norwich, Colchester and Halstead. The Dutch immigrants were skilled in the production of 'bays and says'. They carried on their trade, giving a new impetus to local textile manufacturing and helped to make Essex famous – and wealthy – for its cloth. Bays and says were still known as 'Dutch work' in the mid-seventeenth century.

In 1590, an attempt was made to re-establish the Dutch community in Halstead after 'discourtesies offered them by the townsmen' caused the original settlers to move on to Colchester. Dutch immigrants took over the watermill at Bourne, near Colchester, for weaving white bay and later baize – this was still operating in 1826 but closed by 1840.

As early as December 1622, the Sherriff of Essex reported 'some disquiet among the poor whose livelihood

Saxon archway, All Saints Church, Colchester.

depended on their bay-making' and found that 'unsold cloths were piling up in the sheds of clothiers especially at Coggeshall, Braintree and Bocking'. In 1629, representatives of the Braintree and Bocking weavers approached the quarter sessions to highlight their 'extreme necessytie and disability to maynetaine and relieve themselves and their families'.

Many of the immigrants brought Nonconformist religious beliefs with them, which seemed to strike a chord with the Essex public ... but was not so welcome in high places.

THE SAFFRON BUSINESS

The saffron crocus (*Crocus sativus*) was grown so successfully in Chipping Walden in the sixteenth and seventeenth centuries that the town changed its name to Saffron Walden. The stamens of the saffron flowers were dried over smokeless charcoal fires on haircloth, but the flowers themselves were thrown out into the streets. The stamens were used in medicines, perfume, as a dye and in cooking. Apparently, it could also be used as an aphrodisiac.

By the end of the 1700s, however, saffron was no longer in demand and malt and barley became the main industries in the town. Around 1800, there were over forty maltings just in Saffron Walden itself. Malt was sent to London in large wagons.

THE LOCAL HOP

As Londoners grew wealthy, evidence suggests that they bought land and property in west Essex, either to rent out for additional income or as prestigious homes. Roger Coys had purchased a new house, Stubbers, near North Ockendon in 1563. His son, William (1560–1627), inherited the house and turned the gardens into a showcase for his interest in botany. In the early 1600s, Stubbers was the first place in England to grow tomatoes, ivy-leaved toadflax, Jerusalem artichokes or to see flowering yucca plants.

Probably more interesting to most people was William's success in growing Flemish hops in Britain. He was the first to do so and transformed the brewing industry. William's success spread across the country so that palatable beer could be made more cheaply, with local hops. Almost 100 years later, many of the plants from William's gardens were taken as showpieces for the newly established gardens at Kew. (Incidentally, turnips were first grown in Britain by Dutch and Flemish 'strangers' on their allotments outside Norwich and Colchester.)

DUTCH SEA WALLS

In 1621, the Dagenham and Hornchurch marshes were again flooded due to another breach in the defences. The Dutch engineer, Cornelius Vermuyden, was invited to England to carry out repairs and constructed a barrier which lasted for the next eighty years. Part of Vermuyden's payment was one-third of the drained land. He sold shares in this land, often to fellow Dutchmen and some to French or Walloon Protestants, who then settled in the area as landowners or tenants

Following this success, Henry Appleton of Benfleet asked Vermuyden to assist with reclaiming the marshland around Canvey Island by walling it in. The project was accepted and put under the management of Joas Croppenburg. Again, the payment for the work was one-third of each acre of land reclaimed from the sea.

Croppenburg employed over 300 Dutchmen experienced in the construction of dykes and other sea defences. They successfully reclaimed 3,600 acres (15 square km) with their sturdy walls, backed by a system of dykes and sluices. The south coast of the island, battered by the tidal Thames, was faced with Kentish ragstone. Several of the Dutch workers settled permanently on the island.

But Essex still suffered with flooding. Inundations were recorded in 1663 and 1690. The next really serious tide was on 16 February 1736. The *Gentleman's Magazine* recorded, 'The little isles of Candy [Canvey] and Fowlnesse, on the coast of Essex, were quite under water, not a hoof was saved thereon, and the inhabitants were taken from the upper parts of their houses into boats'.

WINSTANLEY'S LIGHTHOUSE

Henry Winstanley (1644–1703) was born in Littlebury near Saffron Walden. Henry helped to design his own house at Littlebury and he named it 'Little House of Wonders', as it was filled with marvellous inventions of his own.

He became aware of the number of ships and crewmen being lost on the rocks off England's south coast and, against other people's advice, he drew up plans for a lighthouse on Eddystone Rock. His first lighthouse washed away, but he was determined to succeed and built a second, stronger lighthouse on the rock. He was confident of his achievement and deliberately stayed at the lighthouse during a violent storm in 1703. Unfortunately, his confidence was misplaced and both the lighthouse and Henry were washed away. However, his work led others to build subsequent lighthouses which have saved thousands of lives.

NONCONFORMIST BELIEFS

Perhaps the Essex character has always been one of independence and nonconformity. We know its role in the Peasant's Revolt and we have heard of the great numbers burnt for defying the prevailing religious beliefs. On the other hand, perhaps they were easily radicalised by strong leaders and preachers.

Richard Rich, who held the right to appoint priests to dozens of Essex churches, leant heavily towards Protestant beliefs, despite what he told Queen Mary! The vast majority of vicars he appointed had similar beliefs and would have influenced the local populations.

Towns who were not happy with official church services often employed a 'lecturer' to preach to them on Sunday afternoons. John Rogers' father was a shoemaker in Moulsham, but John himself became a lecturer in Dedham. His reputation spread throughout Essex and beyond as 'one of the most awakening preachers of the age'. His nickname of 'Roaring John Rogers' suggests that 'awakening' is meant to be taken literally as well as figuratively. Officials tried to stop his preaching as he did not conform to the *Book of Common Prayer*.

Thomas Hooker (1587–1647) was curate of St Mary's in Chelmsford and acted as a lecturer there from 1626–29. Thomas was among those who decided that they would have more freedom to practise their religion in the new colonies. He went on to become the founder of the state of Connecticut and has been called the 'Father of American Democracy'.

Although people with strong religious beliefs, like Thomas Hooker, have become known as the Founding Fathers of America, it was money that first attracted men from Essex to take an interest in the newly discovered America.

THE *MAYFLOWER* PILGRIMS
Christopher Jones was born in Harwich about 1570. By the age of 30 he was the master of a ship named the *Mayflower*. Christopher and his ship plied the English Channel, exporting English wool to France and importing French wine to London. He also dealt in hats, hemp, hops, salt and vinegar. He had sailed to Norway and maybe even Greenland. Christopher and his ship were a well-travelled pair.

In 1620, Christopher and the *Mayflower* were chartered to take a party of religious families to the new American colonies. Also among the party was Christopher Martin, a Great Burstead churchwarden. He owned a shop in Billericay High Street as well as other property in Great Burstead. He was hired by the pilgrims to take responsibility for purchasing provisions for the journey and help the pilgrims reach the new world safely.

Before long, Robert Cushman, one of the Puritan leaders of the party, wrote of Christopher Martin, '[H]e ... so insulteth over our poor people, with such scorn and contempt, as if they were not good enough to wipe his shoes'. The pilgrims soon learnt that if they questioned Christopher on his decisions or his poor accounting, they received the lash of his tongue.

The *Mayflower*, with 102 passengers, finally left Plymouth bound for the New World on 6 September 1620. Among the crew were John Alden, a 21-year-old cooper, and Richard Gardiner, both from Harwich. John Crackstone and John Jnr came from Colchester and John Guild was another Essex man. Christopher Martin's wife, Mary, and her teenage son from her first marriage, Solomon, were also on board. The Martins also took a 'servant', John Langmore, a 21-year-old from Billericay.

They arrived at Cape Cod on 21 November 1620. They were overcrowded and underfed, not to mention the lack of fresh air and exercise. The sanitary arrangements must have been appalling. That first winter, most of the Essex people died, having hardly set foot on their new promised land. Only three Essex people are known to have survived. Christopher Jones and Richard Gardiner survived the *Mayflower* pilgrimage, although both of them died within the next four years. Young John Crackstone Jnr survived and was fostered by another family. However, in 1627, John Jnr developed a fever after being lost in the woods in freezing weather and died.

THE WASHINGTON LINK

One Essex clergyman who would have been out of place among the New England pilgrims was Lawrence Washington (1602–53), rector of All Saints, Maldon.

During Oliver Cromwell's interregnum, he lost his job as he did not support the Puritan Parliament.

However, Lawrence's son, John (1633–77), born in Purleigh, became involved in the tobacco trade and in 1657 arrived in the colony of Virginia. He liked it and settled there. John's great-grandson, George, became the first president of the new United States of America.

THE WINTHROP FLEET

In March 1629, a group of wealthy merchants led by John Winthrop of Suffolk obtained a royal charter for a colony at Massachusetts Bay. Their fleet of eleven ships, carrying some 700 passengers, arrived in the summer of 1630. A large proportion of the immigrants were from Suffolk but a significant number – between seventy and ninety of them – were from Essex.

Two of John Winthrop's four wives were also Essex girls: Mary Forth of Great Stambridge, and Margaret Tyndal of Great Maplestead. Mary's eldest son, John, was born in Great Stambridge. He followed his father to New England and eventually became a governor of Connecticut. Margaret joined her husband in Massachusetts and helped to establish the new colonies there with very strict Puritan rules.

Others who left Essex on the Winthrop ships were: Edward Convers (1587–1663) of Navestock, who became a wealthy landowner, farmer and miller and helped to found Woburn and Charleston in Massachusetts, and William Pynchon (1590–1662), born in Springfield, who began a very successful fur-trading business in New England, liaising between the American Indians and the settlers. His son, John (1626–1702), was also born in Springfield. By the time John died, he was the wealthiest and most powerful landowner in western Massachusetts.

OTHER NEW ENGLAND NOTABLES

John Haynes (1594–1693) was born in Messing, but later lived at Copford Hall. He became the fifth governor of the

Massachusetts Bay colony. His son, Hezekiah, wrote that his father had invested between £7,000 and £8,000 in the colony 'to the ruine of his famylye in Englande'.

Henry Vane (1613–62) was born in Debden. He arrived at Boston in 1635 and became the sixth governor of the Massachusetts Bay colony. He helped to found Rhode Island, but soon returned to England. He was beheaded on Tower Hill in June 1662 for his support of Cromwell during the Civil War.

By 1640, Samuel Bass's family from Saffron Walden had joined the Massachusetts Bay colony as part of the Great Migration. Also, it was from Chelmsford that the Quaker William Penn left England in 1682 to establish the province of Pennsylvania.

THE CIVIL WAR YEARS

When the English Civil Wars of 1642–53 erupted, the Essex Militia declared for Parliament. With its close proximity to new ideas from London, years of influence from Protestant and Dissenting priests, and influx of Protestants from Holland and France, it was not surprising that Essex would side with the Parliamentarians.

The Parliamentarian's New Model Army, under Sir Thomas Fairfax, made its headquarters at Saffron Walden. Oliver Cromwell, as Lieutenant General of Horse, visited the town in May 1647 and stayed at the Sun Inn. He took a leading role in debates held in the church. These heated discussions aimed to allow Parliament and the army to come to an agreement.

Oliver was familiar with Essex as he had many friends here. His wife, Elizabeth Bourchier, was from Felsted. Her family also owned property at Great Stambridge. Later, two of their sons were educated at Felsted Grammar School, and their youngest daughter, Frances, married Robert Rich of Great Leighs (although he died less than three months after the wedding). Oliver purchased New Hall, Boreham, for his own use during the Commonwealth period.

THE SIEGE OF COLCHESTER

The Lucas boys, Thomas, John and Charles, made their tutors' lives a misery at home in St John's Abbey, Colchester. However, despite their rumbustious behaviour – which involved a great deal of charging noisily around the house, according to their sister's memoires – the boys all attended Cambridge University, were commissioned into the army and eventually knighted by the king.

Their youngest sister, Margaret, proved herself equal in intelligence and flamboyance to any of her brothers. She married William Cavendish and wrote poems, stories and articles about the new scientific discoveries of the day. She was considered eccentric by other ladies and 'mad' by Samuel Pepys, but was the first woman invited to attend a meeting of the Royal Society. Her autobiography is the first ever secular autobiography published by a British woman. She is buried in Westminster Abbey.

All of the Lucas brothers fought for the Royalist cause during the Civil War, but Charles made the most lasting impression on Essex history. Charles Lucas was an enthusiastic leader in the Civil War. Captured by Cromwell's army in 1644, Charles negotiated his release with a promise never to bear arms against the Parliamentarians again. However, four years later, he did just that, leading the Essex Rebellion. After a skirmish in Kent, the Parliamentarian General Thomas Fairfax pursued Charles into Essex. Legend says that Fairfax's troops spent a night in Tilbury church, horses and all, which damaged the church.

Meanwhile, Charles Lucas joined up with Sir George Lisle and Lord Capel at Chelmsford. They led their troops on to Colchester, arriving 12 June 1648, hoping to meet up with reinforcements. When Fairfax arrived, he surrounded the town, cut off supply routes and challenged the Royalists to surrender. The Royalists refused. Three Royalist ships attempted to sail up the River Colne to bring supplies into Colchester but they could not pass the Parliamentarian garrison on Mersea Island. Then, three Parliamentarian ships arrived from Harwich and blockaded the mouth of the Colne.

Puritan Colchester was no doubt furious to be suffering in the siege alongside their enemy. After two months, they all were reduced to eating horses, cats, dogs and straw. The town sent out a party of women and children but Fairfax would not let them leave the shadows of the castle wall and there they were trapped, and starved as quickly as if they had stayed inside the walls.

Starvation killed more people than the cannon and gunfire, although the town still bears the scars of the latter. The besieged Royalists hauled a small cannon to the top of the tower of the Church of St Mary's at the Walls. This tubby little weapon was very effective from its vantage point, and therefore attracted much retaliating fire. Eventually, the tower was damaged to such an extent that the cannon fell down and smashed. This story provided the basis for a new children's rhyme: 'Humpty Dumpty', the Humpty Dumpty being the cannon.

After two and a half months, on 27 August 1648, the Royalists finally surrendered. The terms they accepted were that all would be granted free passage apart from the four senior officers. Two days later, Sir Charles Lucas and Sir George Lisle were stood in front of the castle wall and executed by firing squad.

Despite the town's Parliamentarian sympathies, after the Restoration of Charles II in 1660 Lucas and Lisle's bodies were reinterred in the Lucas family vault in St Giles Church, Colchester, beneath a marble tablet proclaiming that they had been 'in cold blood barbarously murdered'.

Thomas Fairfax who, if he did not order the execution at least condoned it, had Essex links of his own. His wife Anne was an Essex girl, born at Wakes Colne, and was a great-granddaughter of John de Vere, 15th Earl of Oxford. Interestingly, Fairfax's daughter married a Royalist.

For its part in the siege – failing to hand over the Royalists – the town was ordered to pay a £12,000 fine. Half of this money had to be found by the 'stranger community', that is, people who had not been born in England. This gives some indication of the size of the Flemish population of Colchester at the time.

Colchester Castle itself had played no part in the siege as it was already falling to ruin at the time. In 1650, the castle was reported not to be worth the cost of repair.

PARLIAMENTARIANS

Among those outside the town during the siege of Colchester had been Sir Thomas Honeywood of Marks Hall. He had fought bravely for the Parliamentarians and, in 1654, was elected MP for Essex in the first Protectorate Parliament. He was re-elected in 1656 and became a member of Oliver Cromwell's House of Lords in 1657.

Also among the thirteen Essex MPs in 1654 were Sir Henry Mildmay of Little Baddow and Carew Mildmay of Romford. In addition, one member was elected for the Borough of Maldon – Joachim Matthews – and two for Colchester – John Maidstone and Colonel John Barkstead. John Barkstead had, in fact, commanded a regiment at the siege of Colchester and later that year was one of the judges at the trial of Charles I.

At the Restoration in 1660, Barkstead escaped to the continent but was brought back to England and executed. Sir Henry Mildmay, who had also been at Charles I's trial, was imprisoned and later exiled.

WITCH HUNTERS

The Civil War, coming hot on the heels of the disruptive Tudor period, had done nothing to help people feel secure in their religious beliefs. Rural Essex, particularly the remote north-east, was little influenced by the new scientific discoveries being talked of in the London suburbs. Their beliefs were still for the supernatural. Therefore, when Richard Edwards' cow died in Manningtree it was easy to agree that elderly Elizabeth Clarke may well have been responsible.

Local man John Stearne volunteered to find out whether Elizabeth had caused the death by sorcery. By watching the old woman all night, refusing her either food or sleep, he was able to secure a confession. Another local man, a young lawyer called Matthew Hopkins, approved of these methods. Together, the two men decided to help the good people of Essex rid themselves of the witches that lived among them.

Within days of Elizabeth Clarke's confession, John and Matthew had secured confessions from four other women. With these villains safely in Colchester Castle gaol awaiting the assize trials, John and Matthew began to travel through north Essex and into Suffolk, Cambridgeshire and Norfolk seeking out witches. They 'watched' the suspects for as long as it took to secure a confession and employed a woman to 'search' the victims' bodies for warts and blemishes – evidence of suckling evil imps.

In July 1645, twenty witches were hanged at the Norfolk Assizes. Matthew travelled back to give evidence at the Essex Assizes that same month. Twenty women were brought from the squalid cells in Colchester Castle and were questioned before the assize judges in the Sessions House at Chelmsford (since replaced by the Shire Hall). Nineteen women were judged guilty. They were immediately taken to Primrose Hill and hanged. A week later, another eighteen women were hanged at Bury St Edmunds, largely due to the evidence of the self-styled 'witch hunters'.

Over a period of little more than eighteen months about 400 people, mainly old women, were hanged as witches.

Matthew Hopkins, who called himself the 'Witchfinder General'.

Matthew Hopkins alone is thought to be personally responsible for the deaths of 200 of them. After all that hard work, and feeling unwell, Matthew returned to Manningtree. Here, he wrote a pamphlet justifying his actions. However, soon afterwards, he died at home in bed, probably from tuberculosis or a fever contracted in the unhealthy homes of the poor or the fetid gaols in which he incarcerated them. He was still just 27 years old.

QUAKERS AND CONGREGATIONALISTS

Eighteen-year-old James Parnell, a convert to Quakerism, came to Essex in 1655 to preach his religious ideas. He was arrested at Coggeshall in July 1655 and was tried at the Chelmsford Assizes. He refused to pay a fine of £40 and was imprisoned in Colchester Castle. Here, he was kept in a room little larger than alcove. The gaoler provided bread and water, for which James had to climb down a rope from his elevated cell. Eight months after his capture, James fell from the rope and died. However, Quakerism proved popular in Essex and meetings began to be held across the north of the county.

Richard and Mary Cutte are remembered in a magnificent tomb in Arkesden Church, dated 1592. Almost 100 years later, their descendant, also Richard Cutte, allowed the Congregationalists to sign an early covenant at his home, Wodehall, despite their meetings being illegal at that time.

Charles II's 1662 Act of Uniformity was followed by the 'ejection' of any priests who would not accept the new prayer book. Some 114 priests lost their livings in Essex. They included John Ray of Black Notley, who lost his fellowship at Cambridge University but, instead, devoted his life to botany and drew up the world's first scientific scheme for plant classification.

When William and Mary passed the 1689 Toleration Act, the Quakers opened one of the first Friend's Meeting

Houses in Stebbing. Another early chapel was built by the Congregationalists at Bocking in 1707.

THE DUTCH WARS

The Rump Parliament of England's Commonwealth years passed a law in 1651 to limit the carriage of English trade to English ships. This was a direct cause of the subsequent wars with the Netherlands (the Dutch).

A Peace Treaty was signed in 1654, signalling the end of what became known as the First Anglo–Dutch War. However, the next year, Dutch ships blockaded the mouth of the Thames. The plague encouraged them to withdraw, but the war continued. Harwich was in the midst of it all. It was still the principal port for travel to Holland and a packet boat service had been agreed by a postal treaty in 1666. The boats plied between Harwich and Holland twice a week, war or not.

RICHARD HADDOCK AND THE BATTLE OF SOLEBAY

The Battle of Solebay, off the Suffolk coast, marked the beginning of the Third Anglo–Dutch War (1672–74) and saw the loss of the largest and newest ship in the English Fleet, the 100-gun first-rate *Royal James*. Its captain was Richard Haddock of Leigh. On 28 May 1672, the *Royal James* was attacked by Dutch warships and fire boats. Richard fought them off, but his ship was on fire, so he tried to persuade his admiral, Edward Montagu, to abandon ship. Montagu refused but Richard, injured in his foot, jumped into the sea. He attracted the attention of another ship and was rescued. Montagu went down with the *Royal James*.

On his return to London, Richard was called to give an account of the battle to Charles II. This he did and was rewarded with the gift of a silk cap for his part in the battle. He was knighted in 1675 and later became a Member of

Parliament, Controller of the Navy and Commander-in-Chief of the Fleet. For all his high positions, he was unable to secure something he battled for years: financial compensation for the loss of his toe at Solebay.

Sir Richard Haddock was buried in the family tomb at St Clement's, Leigh.

6

GEORGIAN ESSEX: RISING FORTUNES

By 1700 about 130,000 people lived in Essex. Agriculture was still the main occupation, with wheat and corn the main crops. In addition, the cloth industry continued to thrive, particularly in Colchester. Cloth made in Colchester was selling in London for around £30,000 each week. Essex did not immediately or as strongly feel the effects of the Industrial Revolution that was rocking the north of England but was progressing nonetheless.

TURNPIKES AND POSTS

Having no natural stone, early Essex roads were surfaced with gravel at best, or with brushwood to fill in the holes. Court records are full of complaints against villagers for failing in their duty to repair the highways and byways. Visitors too had cause to complain and William Kemp, who danced through Essex on his way from London to Norwich in the spring of 1599, described the road between Chelmsford and Braintree as a 'foul way'. He complained that he 'could find no ease in [it]; thick woods being on either side, likewise being full of deep potholes, sometimes I skipped up to the waist'.

Too late for William Kemp, the Essex Act of 1695–96 formed the Essex Turnpike Trust and called for the London to Harwich road to be repaired. Villagers at Mountnessing were no doubt intrigued to see a toll bar set up across the Great Essex Road as it passed through their village: the first turnpike in Essex. Wagons passing this point paid a shilling, coaches sixpence and horse riders one penny. Mail coaches, soldiers, funeral processions, priests on parish business, prison carts and royalty were exempt from the charges. The turnpike was soon bringing in £400 a year.

The trustees of the turnpike were all Justices of the Peace until 1725 when an independent Turnpike Trust was created, called the Essex Trust. The Middlesex & Essex Trust was responsible for the Great Essex Road from Mile End to Shenfield, where the Essex Trust took over. The Colchester to Dedham road was turnpiked in 1725, and Bishop's Stortford to Cambridge in 1765 under the Essex & Hertfordshire Trust. Between 1695 and 1765, most of the main highways of the county were turnpiked.

Each turnpike was staffed by a lone tollkeeper, who was provided with a small cottage on site. He was on duty twenty-four hours a day, always on alert to open the gate and collect the tolls. The toll gate on the Lea Bridge at Stratford was particularly busy, but elsewhere it could be a lonely job – see Turnpike Lane, West Tilbury, Pool Street Great Yeldam, Fordstreet Hill, Aldham, or Palmers Green, Ugley (the toll houses are no longer there). Often on the remote edges of villages, the toll cottages sometimes provided easy pickings for burglars or highwaymen.

Although far from perfect, the roads were much improved under the care of the trusts. In 1787, the County Surveyor, John Johnson (architect of the Shire Hall) built the current bridge over the Can at Chelmsford, which also improved things for wheeled traffic. However, Arthur

Young was still moved to write in 1768 that 'of all the cursed roads that ever disgraced this kingdom in the very ages of barbarism, none ever equalled that from Billericay to the Kings Head at Tilbury'. Indeed, when the heavy wagons loaded with chalk from the quarries at Purfleet and Stifford became stuck in the mud, it took twenty to thirty horses to pull them out.

At Gun Hill near Dedham, mindful of animal welfare, locals erected a sign condemning the whipping of animals to get them up the hill. They also advised, 'Let not one curse escape your lips. God sees and hears.'

A post (mail) coach service began running from the King's Head at Rochford to Shenfield, three times a week, from 1761. Soon, this was extended to continue all the way to London. By 1762, passengers could ride the new post coach from Harwich to London and back again every day at a cost of threepence a mile. The coaches could travel at up to 10mph, although the average speed was nearer to 3mph.

The Chelmsford coach service set off from the Coach & Horses in the town centre at 7 a.m. and reached the Spread Eagle in London at noon, having changed horses at Romford. Another service ran from Maldon to Whitechapel, three times a week. Coaching inns, where the hired horses were changed, flourished and at one time Colchester had eighty inns.

The drivers, or post-boys, wore the liveries of the inns which employed them. For example, those of the Saracen's Head in Chelmsford wore blue, while those of the White Hart in Brentwood wore red jackets. Post-chaises themselves were often yellow.

At Faulkbourne on the Witham road, the mail coach arrived in the middle of the night and the postmaster, fed up with getting out of bed to receive the post, installed a hatch in his bedroom. The coachman could then reach up and deposit the letters straight into the man's bedroom.

Celebrated locally is Maldon-born Edward Bright whose career as a post-boy ended at the age of 12 when he was already too heavy to ride the ponies. He became a grocer and continued to grow in both size and popularity. Locals joked that 'seven hundred men' could fit inside Edward's waistcoat – this was a pun, referring to seven men from the Dengie hundred.

When he died aged 27, Edward left a thriving business, a wife and six children. The wall of the family home was taken down to enable the huge coffin carrying his 42-stone body to be lifted out with a crane. He was buried at All Saints in Maldon.

A cheaper transport choice for passengers was the regular stage coach service which plied between London and the larger towns, travelling at a steady 5mph. Cheaper still was the option of hitching a ride on a commercial goods wagon. A typical wagon in 1820, loaded with 5 or 6 tons of goods, left London on a Saturday and arrived in Colchester on Monday. If you chose to ride the fish carts from Leigh, the journey was not only bumpy, slow and uncomfortable, but also smelly. The fish carts left Leigh at 6 p.m. and travelled via Wickford to arrive at Billingsgate at 4 a.m.

The increase in traffic was not good news for the county's bridges. For example, the constant maintenance necessary on the bridge on the Southend Road at Wickford led to it being completely rebuilt 1773. The 1820s to 1840s saw the greatest volume of horse-drawn traffic on the roads. In the 1820s, Sir James McAdam was appointed surveyor to the Middlesex & Essex Turnpikes Trust and in 1830 he joined the Epping and Ongar Trust. For them he constructed the Epping New Road through the forest. Then, for all the trusts, including the Essex Turnpikes Trust, which he joined in 1833, he macadamized the roads.

The Essex Turnpike Trust was dissolved in 1866, by which time the takings were much reduced, due to competition from the railways.

CARIBBEAN SLAVES

Like many around the country, Essex merchants and gentlemen took a great interest in the new Caribbean trade. Sugar was a popular investment, although the success of the business depended largely on the use of thousands of slaves transported from Africa to the West Indies. Whether directly involved in this or not, some of Essex's wealth owed much to this slave trade.

Teenaged Franciscus was baptised in Rickling in 1764: 'Feb 3 Franciscus Niger Slave to the Hon'ble and Rev'd Nicholas Boscawen DD, seeming about fourteen years of age.' And a gravestone at Little Parndon (now kept inside the church) remembers Hester Woodley, who died in May 1767, aged 62, for 'discharging her duty with the utmost attention ... in the service of ... Mrs Bridget Woodley to whom she belonged...'. Hester had been brought to Essex from 'the island of St Christopher' (St Kitts) with Bridget.

The eighteenth-century records list several 'slaves', 'blackamoors' and 'Negro servants' in Essex.

DAGENHAM BREACH

Flooding of low-lying coastal areas was an accepted annual occurrence for hundreds of years. An unusually high spring tide in 1707 overtopped the sea wall at Dagenham and flooded into the marshes behind it. Legally, repair was the responsibility of the landowners. However, nobody wanted to take responsibility for mending the breach and so the gap in the sea defences gradually widened. Eventually, after seven years, Parliament intervened and ordered the damage to be repaired at public expense.

Chests full of chalk and sunken ships were unsuccessful at plugging the gap in the river bank and, by 1716, the lake forming behind the sea wall had reached some 150m across and extended nearly 2 miles in length. Then, Captain John

Perry employed 300 men to build sluices into the bank and reinforce it with timber piles. They built a dam where the original breach had occurred and, finally, the opening was effectively controlled, about twelve years after the accident, leaving behind an extensive lake.

In 1887 Samuel Williams built a timber dock at Dagenham Breach with a railway track connected to the mainline. He filled in much of the Breach Lake behind his dock and developed two deep-water jetties. The area became known as Dagenham Dock.

In 1929 construction began on the Ford factory, on concrete piles on part of the reclaimed land. The factory site includes the remains of the Breach Lake today.

It was not until the Land Drainage Act of 1930 that River Boards could levy rates for the maintenance of sea defences from people living beyond the actual flooded area.

SMUGGLING

Smuggling was at its height from 1650–1830, although it had been a way of life for generations. In 1275, Edward I had introduced a custom (tax) on wool exports and by 1614, the export of any wool was officially made illegal. In a wool-producing county like Essex, this presented financial opportunities for 'owlers' – wool smugglers.

Others, such as Henry Parish of Barking, could earn £10 a trip by collecting young priests from remote marshes at Dagenham or Tilbury and taking them across to Europe for training at the Catholic seminaries there; illegal Catholic texts were smuggled into England on the return journey.

Smuggling increased as customs duty was imposed on more and more products. For example, tea was sold at 2*d* in France but priced at 6*d* in England. Almost as soon as tobacco began to be imported from the newly discovered Americas, smugglers found ingenious ways to dry the leaves and hide them in various nooks and crannies in their ships. And as for brandy ... well, that was popular with everyone.

Smuggling became punishable by death by the 1746. However, poor harvests and job losses in Essex in the early 1700s meant that smuggling was often seen as a necessity, rather than a preferred choice. Seventy per cent of wanted smugglers were former labourers. This was not surprising as in one night they could earn seven times the daily wage of a farm labourer.

The *Essex Chronicle* of 10 September 1779 reported on a large, well-armed ship sailing up the Crouch to Hullbridge. Since then, said the paper, 'carts and horses have frequently been seen passing through Danbury, Chelmsford, etc, loaded with goods'. The Maldon customs officers attempted to arrest some of the smugglers but 'they proved too strong for them', although one man died from gunshot wounds received in the skirmish.

Jack Skinner of Colchester, Bessie Catchpole of Harwich and John Bantoft, the 7ft tall 'giant' of Great Clacton, were well known to the authorities, but hundreds of anonymous Essex men made a healthy illicit profit on smuggled goods over the years. The value of goods confiscated in the Port of Colchester amounted to over £1,000 each year.

William Blythe of Paglesham was an oyster dredger, grocer, churchwarden and a smuggler. He was caught more than once by the customs officials but was both clever and lucky. On one occasion, the customs cutter became stuck on the Goodwin Sands. The customs men asked William to get the boat afloat as they knew he was a good sailor. 'I might as well be drowned as hanged,' said William. So, they agreed to free him if he saved the boat and all their lives.

But smuggling was no joke, nor the romantic pastime of fiction. It was hard work, dirty and dangerous. William Dowsett of Leigh, owned the *Neptune* which had a crew of eleven men and six swivel guns. He was spotted in November 1778 on the Crouch with nearly 400 ankers of brandy, rum and gin on board, plus several hundredweight of tobacco, coffee and tea. The customs cutter gave chase and the smugglers only surrendered after two of them were killed.

Similarly, his relative John Dowsett and his boat the *Big Jane* were smuggling tea, gin, rum and brandy in 1780. He was chased for eleven hours before abandoning *Big Jane* and escaping in a smaller boat. It was no coincidence that the haberdashers in Leigh High Street was always well stocked with lace, brocades, silks, tapestries and fancy goods.

Inland parishes were also implicated. Tiptree Heath was a popular hideout for smugglers and their contraband. The Rose at Peldon and the Spread Eagle at Witham both had secret hiding places for smuggled goods. Nearly every church tower around the coast is linked with stories of illicit signalling or storage. However, Essex smugglers tended to work in small groups of locals. They were not associated with the huge bands of ruthless thugs that characterised smuggling in Suffolk, Kent and Sussex.

CUSTOMS OFFICERS

Customs officers were not usually local men, but they became important – if often unpopular – members of the community. The customs service was complex, with the chief officer responsible for searching and seizures of goods, sale of contraband, employees, equipment and mountains of paperwork. The Essex coastline was divided between three customs headquarters: the Port of Colchester, the Port of Maldon and the Port of London.

The Port of Colchester in 1717 employed a collector, a surveyor, a landwaiter, a searcher, two tidesmen, two boatmen at Brightlingsea, a second searcher at Wivenhoe and a boatman at Mersea Island. In addition, boatmen could be hired on a daily rate of pay to supplement the crews when necessary.

On one occasion, a whole boatload of customs men were murdered by smugglers just off the Essex coast. They were buried together beneath their upturned boat in Virley churchyard.

Captain John Harriot (1745–1817) lived at Great Stambridge and, after a colourful life of ups and downs, was asked to give thought to crime on the Thames. He founded the Thames River Police.

In 1845, a new static customs ship, *Watch Vessel No. 7*, was positioned off the coast of Paglesham. In its former life, the ship was known as the *Beagle* and had carried Charles Darwin on his voyage around the Galapagos Islands.

CANALS: THE STOUR, THE LEA AND THE CHELMER

Sea transport continued to be important and rivers were improved to allow boats to travel further inland with their cargoes. The Hythe Quay, for example, was busy with ships loading goods and passengers. The Stour was canalised in 1705, with landing places at Dedham, Langham, Boxted and Wormingford.

In 1797, the Chelmer Navigation Canal opened to link Chelmsford to the Blackwater near Maldon. The canal saw much trade in coal, timber and farm produce, and brought in raw materials for the milling and malting industries.

In west Essex, the River Lea was under the eye of Henry VI's government as early as 1425. Grain for beer and bread travelled on barges to the mills that lined the river. The River Lee Act in 1766 allowed for the river to be made into a canal and for locks to be built. However, encouraging water flow for the benefit of the mills or, alternatively, controlling it with the locks for the benefit of the barge owners was a source of conflict. The Act decreed that the original river would be known as the Lea, while the man-made channel would be the Lee Navigation.

Lord Howard of Audley End objected on more than one occasion to plans for a canal between Bishop Stortford and Cambridge as it would pass too near to his house. The scheme had to be abandoned.

The Lee Conservancy Board took ownership of the Stort Navigation Company in 1905. Locks were rebuilt in the 1920s and flood relief improvements were built in the 1930s. However, commercial traffic began to decline on the river and it was given over to holiday and leisure use in the 1970s. The canal system was nationalised in 1947 and it is now under the control of British Waterways.

OYSTERS: NORTH AND SOUTH

As early as 1566 there were concerns about the overfishing of oysters at Colchester. It was agreed that oysters could not be caught between Easter and September and that they could only be sold from the Hythe Quay. Mersea and Brightlingsea gradually came to dominate the fisheries, and Colchester obtained an Act of Parliament around 1740 to appoint three magistrates and twelve dredgermen to supervise the oyster industry and protect their interests.

Oysters also flourished in the Thames Estuary and were instrumental in the growth of a new town at the south end of Prittlewell. When local fishermen realised the profits to be made from fattening oysters in prepared beds, or 'layings', that could be cleaned with each rise and fall of the tide, they built a cluster of cottages on the shore to be near their new oyster layings. Soon, an inn and a terrace of brick properties lined the seafront and people shortened the name of the settlement from 'the south end of Prittlewell' to just 'Southend'.

Kent fishermen noticed the high prices the Essex oysters attracted and 500 Kentish men raided the shore at Southend one day in 1724. The Southend men protested aggressively but the Kent men said that anything found in the sea was there for the taking. The case went before the local magistrates who found in favour of the Essex men. Kent had to pay an enormous fine.

DICK TURPIN

Richard 'Dick' Turpin was born in 1705 to John and Mary Turpin of the Rose and Crown Inn (now called the Bluebell) in Hempstead. Apprenticed to a butcher, Dick could have led a respectable life. However, he became involved with the Gregory Gang, who made money where they could with smuggling, poaching, burglary and highway robberies.

News reports recount how the gang tied up householders while they robbed properties. On one occasion, Dick held a woman over her own fireplace for refusing to reveal where she kept her money. He was no charming rogue, more a ruthless thug. He was a wanted man with a price on his head.

Later, Dick teamed up with Matt 'Tom' King to rob passing coaches in the Epping area. One day, they were involved in a tussle with some constables. Dick fired a shot and Tom fell dead. We shall never know whether Dick was deliberately aiming to silence his partner or to kill the constables. However, now a murderer, Dick hid in a secret cave in Epping Forest while the price on his head rose to £200 – a fortune.

A forest keeper discovered the hideout and decided to capture Dick and claim the reward. He was well armed with his own loaded hunting rifle and called for Dick to come out of the cave and give himself up. There was a rustle in the bushes and a shot rang out – the forest keeper received a bullet in the stomach and died in agony.

With two murders to his name, Dick had no option but to escape. He rode to Lincolnshire and then on to York (not in a single day, however, nor on a horse named Black Bess). In York, Dick posed as a respectable horse trader named John Palmer – little did his customers realise the horses were stolen property. One day, Dick shot a cockerel. It was a joke to Dick but a tragedy to the bird's owner, who had him arrested. In jail, Dick was worried that his true identity would be discovered and he wrote to his brother-in-law at Hempstead for a character reference. Not recognising the name and unwilling to pay the required postage, the brother-in-law returned the letter to the main post office at Saffron Walden. There, Dick's handwriting was recognised by his former schoolmaster. The schoolmaster contacted the magistrates, enquiries were made, Dick was exposed, and the trial at York became significantly more interesting.

Despite Dick's crimes, a lack of evidence saw him convicted only of stealing a mare, but the penalty was the same as it would have been for the murders and Dick was hanged at York in April 1739.

NEW LEASE OF LIFE FOR COLCHESTER CASTLE

John Wheeley purchased Colchester Castle in 1683 for its sheer size. He began to demolish it and to sell off the stone. Luckily, he had not removed much of the building before he sold it on to the Creffield family. Later, it came into the ownership of Charles Grey (1696–1782), who roofed the castle with red tile, built the round turret and purchased the castle grounds. Charles Grey also planted some holly trees in Colchester in the garden of a house he owned, now known as the Hollytrees Museum.

Charles' step-granddaughter from his wife's first marriage inherited the castle and she and her husband later sold it to Viscount Cowdray, a former MP for the town. He gave the building to the Borough of Colchester as a museum and to stand as a memorial to the First World War.

A NEW SHIRE HALL

The people of Chelmsford rebuilt their Sessions House at the head of the marketplace around 1569. They met there to trade at the corn market as well as for the important assize courts and county quarter sessions. The Shire Hall

Chelmsford Shire Hall, designed by John Johnson, the county surveyor, and opened in 1791.

replaced the Sessions House in 1791, after more than ten years of discussions, arguments and negotiations.

The second floor of the new building included an assembly room with a music gallery. Here, the middle and upper classes came to enjoy balls, meetings and social events. The large room was also used as the courtroom if there were numerous prisoners to be tried. The usual two court rooms were downstairs with other administrative offices. Part of the ground floor was an open area used as the corn exchange. However, this was eventually found to be unpopular. Merchants found the light too dim to be able to inspect the corn and, therefore, a new corn exchange was built nearby in 1857.

The Shire Hall has undergone many alterations, but the assembly room is still the largest ballroom in Essex.

THE RISE AND FALL OF WANSTEAD HOUSE

The royal hunting lodge at Wanstead was popular with all the Tudor monarchs. Later, James I visited several times and drank the water for his health – despite advice that others had died from doing so. In fact, a spa was established at Wanstead in 1619 when it came into private ownership.

Sir Henry Mildmay had to forfeit the estate for siding with Parliament during the Civil War and Sir Josiah Child began to improve the estate in 1680s. When John Evelyn visited in 1683, he wrote, 'I went to see Sir Josiah Child's prodigious cost in planting walnut trees about his seate, and making fish ponds many miles in circuit in Epping Forest, in a barren place'.

However, it was the next generation, Sir Richard Child, who transformed the manor house into a Palladian mansion between 1715 and 1722. Its portico had six Corinthian columns, the first to be seen in England, and the grounds were landscaped by George London. It was a truly magnificent residence.

When Catherine Tylney-Long inherited Wanstead House along with the rest of her family's fortune in 1805, she became the richest heiress in England. Unfortunately, Catherine chose an extravagant, irresponsible and unfaithful husband: William Wellesley-Pole, a nephew of the Duke of Wellington. The family name became Pole-Tylney-Long-Wellesley. William ran through Catherine's fortune in no time and soon creditors were clamouring for money. Under the terms of a will, the estate could not be sold for 1,000 years, so a month-long auction saw all Catherine's inheritance and beautiful possessions sold. Three years later, in 1825, the house which had cost around £360,000 to build was demolished and sold as building material for £10,000. Poor Catherine was then abandoned by her husband and died of an illness shortly afterwards.

The Corporation of London bought 184 acres (0.74 square km) of Wanstead Park from Wellesley's heir to preserve as a part of Epping Forest, and the resultant new municipal park of Wanstead was officially opened in 1882. The last two of the walnut trees planted by Josiah Child in

1683 died in the 1980s. By that time, the largest measured 40ft (12m) high and over 7ft (2.29m) around its trunk.

LANDSCAPE DESIGNS

Mapmakers Chapman and Andre travelled across the whole of Essex in 1777 mapping the landscape. Their maps show a rolling, open countryside dotted with manor houses with relatively small, enclosed parks. Essex and Kent were unusual in being almost totally enclosed by 1600. Most fields were enclosed direct from the forest without passing through the open field stage at all. The 1801 Enclosure Act enabled villages where three-quarters of the landowners agreed to enclose any remaining open fields and common land, allocating ownership to a few landowners.

A fashion for artificial but natural-looking parks began among landowners in the 1730s. Lancelot 'Capability' Brown (1716–83) was in demand by estate owners to landscape their grounds in the modern style. His influence can still be seen at Audley End, Belhus, Navestock and Thorndon Hall, even where the house itself has disappeared.

The 1st Baron Petre had remodelled Old Thorndon Hall during the 1570s. The 8th Baron, Robert Petre (1713–42), decided it needed an update and he drew up detailed plans for extensive and magnificent grounds surrounding the house. His plans included exotic plants from around the world and modern heated glasshouses (known as 'stoves') to grow pineapples, bananas, guavas, papayas and limes. His dream was to create a botanical estate to rival any in England.

He made a start, and Thorndon Hall saw the first camellia ever to flower in Britain. Robert planted over 60,000 trees of more than fifty different varieties. There are rumours that his enthusiasm for nature led him to import foreign wildlife too. Some say we have Lord Petre to thank for introducing the first grey squirrels into Essex, which subsequently destroyed our native red squirrel population.

Unfortunately for the gardens, Robert died of small-pox (along with thirty members of his family) before his plans could come to anything and his son had no interest in gardening or landscaping. However, the 9th Lord Petre was interested in the house. He hired James Paine who designed a completely new hall. The new mansion was built between 1764 and 1770. Capability Brown's landscape design was the crowning glory: 1,000 acres of parkland with two lakes.

HUMPHRY REPTON

Nearly as famous as Capability Brown, Humphry Repton also found work in Essex. In fact, he came to live at Hare Street in Romford, now renamed Main Road, in Gidea Park. His influence is more widely seen in this county than Brown's. For example, Repton worked at Blake Hall, Ongar, Dagnam Park, Havering and Hill Hall, Epping.

During 1797, Humphry worked on transforming the 41-acre gardens of a house near Chelmsford called Highlands (Hylands). The house itself had been built in 1728. Humphry's designs included a serpentine lake, pleasure gardens and far-reaching vistas. In 1966, Chelmsford Borough Council purchased the estate and restored the park to reflect Humphry's vision.

Humphry helped Wellesley run through his wife's fortune at Wanstead Park with grand new designs for the grounds. Nearby, he drew up the designs for Highams Park, Woodford, and the grounds of Warren House, Loughton. Also in the county, Humphry worked on Copped Hall and Gosfield Place. His influence can be seen at Harewood House and at Warley Woods.

In 1814 the owner, William Russell, asked Humphry to suggest alterations for Stubbers House and gardens. Humphry produced a 'Red Book', which still exists today, although his plans were never used. Humphry Repton died in 1818 at his home in Hare Street.

AUDLEY END

Thomas Audley's grandson, Thomas Howard, was made 1st Earl of Suffolk, Baron of Walden, and appointed as Lord Chamberlain and later Lord Treasurer to James I. Thomas rebuilt Audley End house on the site of Walden Abbey in an elaborate style and commissioned a young employee, Henry Winstanley, to produce some etchings of the house and estate. Later, Thomas Howard lost his positions due to suspected embezzlement, and then had great difficulty maintaining his enormous mansion.

Charles II bought the house in 1667 for £50,000, although the Howards were allowed to remain in residence in a small part of it as 'keepers' of the property. Just a few years later, the king sold the house back to the family. For convenience and financial reasons, the Howards began to take down parts of the property built by their extravagant ancestor.

Elizabeth, Countess of Portsmouth, inherited the house in 1751 and continued this trend, demolishing the long gallery and reducing other parts of the building to a single storey. Elizabeth's heir, Sir John Griffin Griffin, employed Robert Adam to add galleries to connect the two sides of the house. Sir John also added a new suite of ground-floor reception rooms on the south front, a flamboyant state apartment on the first floor and restored the north and south wings to their original height. Outside, meanwhile, Lancelot 'Capability' Brown remodelled the grounds.

Sir John was interested in technology and commissioned a water pump on the Cam to provide piped water in the house. Five water closets were personally installed by their inventor; the equivalent cost in today's money was over £1,000 each. He installed a complicated system of wires to provide bell pulls in all the major rooms, connecting to bells in the servants' quarters – some of the first installed in England. Furthermore, he invested in a new-fangled lighting system with oil lamps which provided light equivalent to ten candles.

Sir John died without direct heirs, and so the Braybrook family inherited Audley End.

FOOD RIOTS

Methodist preacher John Wesley described Essex as 'an extremely pleasant and fruitful farming area' in 1758. However, when William Pitt visited Essex in 1795 he said that he had had no idea that there was 'a spectacle of such misery' in any part of England. The reason was food shortages brought about by a series of poor harvests and, of course, the French wars which disrupted imports. Prices soared during the hostilities and a farmer from Herongate near Brentwood claimed to have established a record price for selling grain. The purchasers, of course, were not as delighted as the sellers.

The authorities held meetings in many towns, and at Saffron Walden they resolved:

> Every expedient should be used for lessening the consumption and eking out the supply [of flour]; the inhabitants present do thereupon resolve to use in their own families a coarser sort of flour, and a small a quantity of it as possible, using every substitute that can be devised.

A system of tickets was set up, whereby the poorest inhabitant could buy bread at lower prices, and Lord Howard agreed to subsidise the purchase of flour for the town. However, people's resentment grew with their hunger.

On 7 July 1795, the mayor of Saffron Walden, Henry Archer, wrote to Lord Howard (Sir John Griffin Griffin) to say:

> A very alarming riot has taken place here in consequence of the high price of provisions ... the civil power of the place will not be sufficient to quiet the disturbance without the aid of the military.

In fact, a mob had marched up the street protesting about high food prices; they had forced their way into shops, taking food and paying the prices they chose. Similar food riots broke out at Colchester, Boreham, Harlow and Halstead. Flour mills were attacked and corn shipments were prevented from leaving the county.

Lord Howard took his responsibilities seriously and arranged for some military assistance. Then, no doubt, he went home to Audley End, used his flushing toilet, rang his state-of-the-art bell for his servant, and sat down beside his bright new oil lamp to contemplate his expensive Temple of Concord and professionally designed Elysian Garden.

Meanwhile, in the village, two troops of Light Dragoons arrived from Colchester to restore order among the hungry crowds. They made their presence felt at Braintree, Thaxted and Saffron Walden, where further riots were feared.

Soon, over 1,000 people a week were receiving handouts of bread at Saffron Walden, Romford, Epping and Chelmsford. A third of the population of Terling received flour, rice and herrings. Elsewhere, for example at Colne Engaine, Black Notley and Ingatestone, labourers with large families were given cash payments. Reverend John Howlett of Great Dunmow wrote that the condition of the poor was 'worse than ever' due to the 'inadequacy of earnings'. Poor relief expenditure rose to about £2 per head and was much higher in rural Essex than in the towns.

A survey in the early 1800s found 212 windmills in Essex but there was not enough corn for them to grind. It was an ongoing problem and in June 1800 labourers in Southminster

and Steeple organised a strike of all work in the Dengie.
Shipments of food were seized at Harwich, fires were started
at Braintree and threatening letters were sent to millers and
shopkeepers in Great Bardfield and Saffron Walden.

In the south of the county, where there was more dairy
farming and sheep grazing on the marshes, conditions were
not so desperate. Wages were more reliable because sheep
and dairy farming was not dependent on the weather like
the wheat fields in the north of the county.

Mountnessing windmill. This post-mill was built in 1807, replacing several
earlier mills on the same site.

MARKET GARDENING ON THE LONDON BORDERS

With an ever-increasing number of mouths to feed, London too was demanding greater quantities of fresh produce and looked towards neighbouring Essex. The towns bordering London found they could harvest salad crops and sell them in London within a day. Therefore, from 1780, market gardening developed along the Lea Valley and increased through the 1800s.

Dagenham residents had grown reeds for centuries on the marshes, for thatching and hurdles. The reed ground was some 100 acres of land in 1700 but was in decline throughout the century. Instead (sometimes as well), Dagenham began to grow vegetables for the London market. The disafforestation of Hainault Forest provided more land for cultivation, which increased the output.

The market gardens were well placed to be fertilised by London sewage, often brought by barge along the river.

FRENCH WARS AND MARTELLO TOWERS

France declared war on England on 1 February 1793, although official news of that fact did not reach London for another two weeks. The Essex coast was considered vulnerable to invasion and so additional defences were immediately suggested. New infantry barracks were built at Colchester in 1794.

Between 1796 and 1798, thirteen semaphore signal stations were established around the coast from Shoeburyness to Harwich. In addition, military camps were set up at Purfleet, Tilbury, Warley, Galleywood Common, Danbury, Sewers End, Littlebury Beacon, Lexden and Bradfield Heath.

At the same time, Essex was called upon to provide 316 men for the navy. Moves were made to encourage recruits to the regular army at the expense of the local militias.

However, Britain's political situation with four changes of government between 1801 and 1807 caused frequent changes in recruitment priorities.

Napoleon restarted the war in May 1803 and Essex felt the threat of invasion even more. In 1805, a series of twenty-nine Martello towers (named for a round fort in Mortella, Corsica) were constructed between Brightlingsea and Aldeburgh. The towers were given identifying letters: A to Z, plus AA, BB and CC. The towers were supported by a circular Redoubt Fort at Harwich, built of brick and granite in 1808. It was designed to be bombproof and was remodelled in 1861 to house ten 24-pounder cannon.

Each Martello tower could accommodate thirty men under siege conditions. However, due to the army's concern about 'the unhealthiness of the coast', the men – three men and a sergeant for each Martello – lived at Weeley Barracks and marched 10 miles from there to Clacton, and so on, every day.

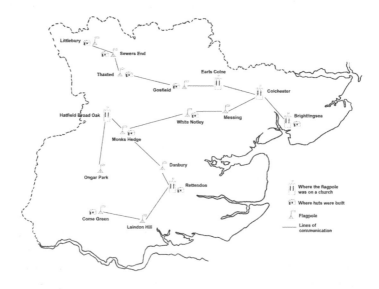

Early warning signal stations, 1808. Each signal was to be guarded 'by some careful person near the spot' for 3s a week.

Weeley Barracks itself was built in 1803, with timber buildings on brick foundations. Several regiments were stationed there during the war, including the 79th, 1st Battalion Cameron Highlanders, 59th, 2nd Battalion East Lancashires and 10th Lincolnshires.

Of the eleven Essex Martello towers (B to K), five have been demolished. The remaining six are now Grade II listed. Tower A at St Osyth opens to the public as a museum and Tower F at Clacton is a restaurant.

ROYAL GUNPOWDER MILLS, WALTHAM ABBEY

A fulling mill on the River Lea set up by the monks at Waltham Abbey was converted into a vegetable oil mill in the early seventeenth century. It transformed in 1665 into a site for the production of gunpowder in response to demand arising from the Dutch Wars. Thomas Fuller, a historian, inspected the mills in 1735 and declared them to be 'the largest and compleatest works in Great Britain'. Many agree that the efficiency of the mills played a significant role in Britain's military successes.

CAROLINE OF BRUNSWICK

The first record of sea bathing at Southend dates from 1768 but it did not take off as a resort at that time. When Caroline of Brunswick, wife of the Prince Regent (later George IV), visited the new resort of 'South-end' (the south end of Prittlewell parish) in 1805 she took three of the grand properties in Royal Terrace to accommodate herself and her entourage. It was noted that when Captain Thomas Manby moored his ship off Southend and visited Caroline there, he did not leave until the following morning. Notwithstanding the rumours of impropriety, Southend celebrated and advertised the royal visit, as it put the new town on the map as a genteel watering place.

Evidence from the Southend holiday was produced fifteen years later when the prince accused his wife of adultery. Essex was on the side of the queen, and in court Judge Nicholas Conyngham Tindal (born in Moulsham in 1776) successfully defended her. It was he who reformed English criminal law to introduce the verdict of 'not guilty by reason of insanity', and the defence of 'provocation' to reduce a murder verdict to manslaughter.

Caroline was not a lucky lady. In August 1821, just three weeks after her husband had been crowned George IV, she died. Essex turned out in force to pay respects to the funeral procession that passed through the county from London to Harwich. *The Times* reported that a 'large concourse of people' had gathered at Harwich Harbour to witness the queen's coffin embark for Germany. As the coffin was lowered into the boat, guns began firing from Landguard Fort and the salute was taken up by the moored ships of war, continuing until sunset.

MALDON ELECTIONS

Across England before 1832 only men who owned land worth over 40s were allowed to vote. By 1800, this equated to about one in seven men in Essex. Essex was represented in Parliament by two knights of the shire, while the three boroughs, Colchester, Maldon and Harwich, each had two Members of Parliament.

On election day, the candidates would arrive at Chelmsford in their carriages from all parts of the county. Dressed in their finest, they stood on a platform in the High Street and made their speeches, while the voters (also arrived from all over Essex) publicly declared their support, to the cheers and boos of the crowd. Free beer was provided at the expense of the candidates. No doubt the occasion was welcomed by the innkeepers more than by the constables of Chelmsford.

In the Borough of Harwich, the mayor and the select few aldermen entitled to vote usually favoured the candidate who promised them lucrative or prestigious government jobs, such as Collector of Customs. The same system operated elsewhere, which explains why Thomas Mildmay of Chelmsford was elected as MP for Lostwithiel in Cornwall (1563–67), and William Heygate of Southend became MP for Sudbury in Suffolk (1818–26).

In Colchester and Maldon, most of the freemen – male property owners over the age of 21 – had the right to vote. Although there was some conferring of voting rights that was not strictly above board, it is thought that the Colchester elections mostly gave a true reflection of the feelings of the borough residents.

In Maldon, however, it was possible to acquire the rights of 'freeman of the borough' by gift, purchase or inheritance. Therefore, many men with voting rights did not actually live in Maldon. Candidates, of course, made the most of this, selling voting rights to their supporters from elsewhere and spending fortunes on finding and transporting voters into the borough on election day. The 1826 elections saw the three candidates spend nearly £50,000 between them on proving the voting rights of men from across Essex, Cambridgeshire, Suffolk, Hertfordshire and even further afield. The poll was open daily from 7–23 June 1826 and the Mayor of Maldon made sure it shut early when Whig supporters were coming from London, but opened later when Tory voters were on their way.

Such practices were well known to the government, who brought in the Reform Act in 1832 in an attempt to create a system that was less open to abuse. A further Act in 1884 divided Essex into eight divisions which could elect one member each, plus West Ham which could elect two members.

Secret voting by ballot came in with the 1870 Ballot Act, and the Corrupt Practices Act of 1883 stamped out much of the bribery and corruption at elections. This growth of democracy led to the rise of a third political party: the Labour Party. In 1892, James Keir Hardie, representing West Ham South, became the first Labour Member of Parliament.

HARWICH: LIGHTHOUSES AND PACKET BOATS

A pair of brick lighthouses protected Harwich Harbour in 1818, replacing the original wooden ones. The taller, nine-sided lighthouse in the main street was 90ft high, with seven floor levels inside. The shorter lighthouse, on the foreshore, was half the height and had ten sides. They came as a pair so that boats could navigate by keeping the higher light visible directly above the lower light. They ceased to operate in 1863 when the course of the channel shifted and, in turn, were replaced by iron lighthouses at Dovercourt.

The Post Office had thirteen sailing vessels on permanent hire at Harwich in 1828. Nine of them sailed between Harwich and Helvoetsluys (Hellevoetsluis), and four between Harwich and Gothenburg. Customs officials were kept busy searching pockets and clothes of passengers. However, a guinea in the right hand and assurances that goods were for one's own use could assure a less strict examination. Others found they were searched at Harwich, then again when they reached Manningtree and once again when they arrived in London.

Around the 50 miles of Essex coastline, the packet boats and fishing boats mingled with barges, merchant ships, tug boats, lightermen, cutters and yachts, to name but a selection of the craft belonging to Essex. Sailors and old sea salts lived and worked on board, often with their wives, daugh-

Harwich High and Low lighthouses, which operated as a pair from 1818 to 1863. They were replaced by cast iron lighthouses on Dovercourt seafront.

ters, mothers and grandmothers, who contributed as much to the family business as the men.

Reverend Arthur Pertwee began to record the names of local men lost at sea in 1872 on tiles decorating his church of All Saints at Brightlingsea. In March 1883, nineteen names were added to his list when a gale swallowed three fishing smacks.

7

VICTORIAN ESSEX: UPS AND DOWNS

By the time Queen Victoria was crowned in 1837, there were over 300,000 people living in Essex. According to the 1811 census, 54 per cent of the population of Essex was employed in agriculture (200 years later, it is about 1.3 per cent). During Victoria's reign, Britain was transformed by a national railway network and increased mechanisation of industry. By the end of her life, the effects of improved health care and education systems were benefiting almost everyone.

BARKING'S FISHERY

Many Essex coastal towns depended heavily on the fishing industry from 1300 to 1850, although most fishermen worked independently or in family groups. Daniel Defoe noted that small 'fisher boats come at every tide' to the Maplin Sands for their daily catch.

Saltwater fishing from Barking was mentioned as early as 1320, when its fishermen were prosecuted for using nets with too small a mesh. Records from the 1660s show Barking had fourteen fishing smacks, crewed by seventy men and boys.

Scotsman Scrymgeour Hewett (1765–1840) moved to Barking as a young man, married a local girl and began to grow his father-in-law's fishing business. As a sideline, Scrymgeour kept a larger, armed ship for casual privateering against Britain's enemies' ships. Under Scrymgeour's son, Samuel, the family business, known as the Short Blue Fleet, grew to become the largest fishing fleet in Britain, at its height comprising 220 boats.

Samuel realised that by packing the fish in ice and using smaller, faster cutters to ferry the catch back to port, the fishing boats could stay out at sea for between three to six months. This was the secret of his success. New ice was continuously delivered to the fishing boats. It was made by flooding the Barking marshes every winter and then 'harvesting' the resulting ice. Thousands of tons of ice could be stored right through the summer.

By 1860, most Barking residents were involved in fishing, either as fishermen or in the supply or distribution trades. Samuel relocated the Short Blue Fleet to Suffolk in 1862 and a huge storm killed sixty Barking fishermen the following year. On top of those disasters, the railway cancelled out Barking's advantage of being located near London. Some families followed the fleet to Suffolk, others found alternative work. By 1870, only three fishing smack owners were listed in Barking and by 1900 it was no longer a fishing port at all.

COURTAULD'S

At harvest time, agricultural labourers could earn 2s a day (double the usual rate) plus free beer and a meal; in the winter, there may have been no work at all. However, women could earn 1s 6d a day for spinning all through the year. This more reliable income encouraged families to seek work in the cloth industries. Although the woollen industry declined from the 1770s, weavers at Bocking, Braintree and Halstead took up silk weaving and continued their cottage industries.

George Courtauld and his cousin Peter Taylor began a silk mill at Pebmarsh in 1794. Reasonably successful, George retired to America twenty years later and left his business to his son, Samuel. It was Samuel who expanded and modernised the business, installing machinery in the factory and by 1818 opening two additional factories: at Bocking and Halstead. By 1835 he had 106 power looms at Halstead Mill.

Over 90 per cent of Samuel's workforce was female, some under 10 years old. The reason – adult males at Courtauld's mills were paid 7*s* 2*d* a week, women were paid up to 5*s* a week, but girls under 11 years old could be paid as little as 1*s* 5*d* a week.

While Samuel supported the 1832 Reform Act, he was not so enthusiastic about the 1833 Factory Act. Samuel objected to the law 'interfering' with his business, saying, 'No children among the poor in this neighbourhood are more healthy than those employed in factories'. For the times, he was considered a sympathetic employer and Samuel was proud of the cottages he built for his workers.

Over the next fifty years, the company's profits rose over 1,000 per cent and from 1850 it employed over 2,000 people. However, men working in the factories were lucky if they earned £30 a year. Samuel's own annual income was £46,000 when he purchased Gosfield Hall as his new home. He refused to negotiate with his power-loom workers when they went on strike at Halstead in 1860 and told his foreman, 'Report to me the names of the 20 to 50 of those who have been foremost in this shameful disorder, for immediate and absolute discharge'.

Increasingly deaf, but still with a controlling hand on his business, Samuel died in 1881. His fortune was left to his adopted daughter, Louisa, but his nephews took over the business, overseeing its rise to become an international player. It was Samuel's great-nephew, also called Samuel, who founded the Courtauld Institute of Art in London.

POOR LAW AMENDMENT ACT 1834

Elizabeth I's Poor Laws served the country virtually unchanged for 250 years, with the old, sick, orphaned or unemployed reliant on their village poor relief rates and individual charitable donations. The cost of poor relief in Essex rose sharply after 1750. In 1775, it totalled £74,067, but in 1815 it amounted to £226,252. This is partly explained by the agricultural depression causing higher food prices, a sharp rise in unemployment, fewer apprenticeships in the declining cloth trade and the Napoleonic Wars. Dunmow spinners were earning 8*d* a day in 1750 but only 4*d* by 1790.

Despite the emergency measures of bread allowances were introduced after the Saffron Walden riots in 1795. Costs continued to escalate. For example, Great Clacton's bill rose from £922 in 1816 to £1,558 in 1817; Beaumont-cum-Moze's rose from £433 to £719 over the same period.

So-called 'outdoor relief' schemes were decided on a case-by-case basis. David and Sarah Rivenall, Chelmsford-born but living in London, wrote over thirty letters to the Chelmsford Vestry (the parish administration committee) between 1824 and 1829 as the family could not survive on David's earnings. Their two daughters could not obtain work as they were 'prevented for want of clothing'. Twice David was imprisoned for debt and the family were turned out of their home for non-payment of rent. One of their baby twins died and another child was lost to measles soon afterwards. The total cost for the funeral (one coffin between the two children) came to £2 9*s*, towards which the Chelmsford Vestry paid only £1.

Larger parishes had experimented with larger work-houses before. Walthamstow, for example, had erected a purpose-built workhouse in 1730: a two-storey design with eight rooms accommodating thirty to forty inmates and enlarged in 1756. Above the door, they had inscribed, 'If any would not work, neither should he eat'. Similarly, Barking had built a workhouse in 1788 for £4,000 and inscribed above their front door, 'This house of Industry at the sole expence of the inhabitants of Barking is to provide and protect the industrious and punish the idle and wicked'.

Individual schemes for communal workhouses had not been very successful – a new, universal system was agreed with the establishment of the Poor Law Commission under the Act of 1834. Essex was divided into seventeen 'unions'. These varied in size from seven to thirty-five parishes. Six small parts of Essex joined up with Suffolk, Cambridgeshire, Middlesex or Hertfordshire Unions. One man from each parish was elected to serve on the boards of guardians, and purpose-built workhouses became a prominent feature of the main towns in the unions. For example, Walthamstow became part of the West Ham Union, with a new workhouse built in 1839–41 in Leyton.

The Epping workhouse was built for £6,000 to house 220 paupers, segregated by age and sex. Here, the dining hall doubled as a chapel on Sundays. The Braintree guardians, however, refused to employ a chaplain, arguing that a walk to the parish church provided the only outing for the inmates.

John Castle lost his job as a Coggeshall silk weaver due to the depression and was forced to seek accommodation at the Witham Workhouse. On admission, he followed the advice of a friend to put his name down as 'Dissenter', although he had been brought up in the Anglican Church. The reason was that the parish church was close to the door of the workhouse but the chapel was a long walk, which he looked forward to every Sunday.

The workhouse guardians had their own problems, as the workhouses were often stretched to their limit. To reduce numbers the guardians encouraged migration, for example to the mills of Yorkshire and Lancashire, but this was very unpopular.

The Romford Workhouse had to find accommodation for 9,540 'tramps' in 1899, and Colchester had over 4,000 in 1906. Billericay tried to discourage vagrants asking for admission with hard labour (stone breaking) and a bread and water diet. Regular inmates enjoyed 7 ounces of bread and a pint of gruel six days a week, with beef and vegetables on Sundays. One hopes they made exceptions for the likes of Ada Cousins, a 25-year-old pea picker from Suffolk who was walking to Braintree with 2-year-old Rose and Charles, who was just 6 months old.

By the turn of the nineteenth century, some of the stricter workhouse rules began to be relaxed and treatment more sympathetic. The Romford board of guardians, for example, built a dedicated infirmary in 1891.

The Chelmsford Union opened separate homes for pauper children in 1906: one for boys at Writtle and one for girls at Great Baddow. At Tendring for Christmas 1908, two men travelled from Frinton to show a series of 'cinematographic pictures' to the workhouse inmates. Everywhere, Christmas Day rations (roast meat followed by plum pudding) were allowed on the day of Queen Victoria's jubilees in 1887 and 1897, and at the coronations in 1902 and 1911.

After the 1845 Asylum Act, every county was required to provide an asylum. Essex commissioned a new building

Warley Hospital, opened in 1853 as the Essex County Lunatic Asylum. It closed in 2001.

large enough to accommodate 450 inmates and it opened at Warley in 1853.

RAILWAYS

Charles Dickens was forced to make an overnight stop in Chelmsford in 1835 as the railway at that time did not allow him to travel all the way from London to Ipswich. He wrote to a friend, 'If anyone were to ask me what in my opinion was the dullest and most stupid spot on the face of the Earth, I should decidedly say Chelmsford.' His frustration with the town arose from his inability to find a newspaper on a Sunday. Luckily for Charles, the railway service soon transformed Essex no less than it did the rest of Britain.

On 20 June 1839, the first section of the Eastern Counties Railway (ECR) opened between Mile End and Romford. Brentwood was connected by 1840, and by early 1843 you could travel all the way to Colchester. Three years later, you could continue your journey to Ipswich on the Eastern Union Railway (EUR).

Detailed surveys of the lines were commissioned from leading surveyors and sometimes had to be carried out in secrecy to avoid arousing local protests. Landowners such as Lord Petre of Ingatestone Hall made sure they had their say over where the stations would be located.

Robert Stevenson designed the Great Eastern Railway from London to Colchester. The Great Eastern took over both the ECR and the EUR in 1862, and train passengers could journey to Maldon, Braintree and Chelmsford, where the station had already been completely rebuilt. Braintree's station was rebuilt in brick in 1869 when the line opened from Bishop Stortford.

The EUR developed other local railways, including the Manningtree–Harwich line which opened in 1856. They also financed the short-lived Colchester, Stour Valley, Sudbury and Halstead Railway. Peter Bruff, who designed

Chappel Viaduct, was the chief engineer on the line. The viaduct at Chappel was describe as 'stupendous' when it first opened. It runs 80ft above the River Colne and is made up of thirty-two brick arches.

At the marshy Ray Island, off Harwich, the railway company created Parkeston Quay in 1883. The quay laid the foundations for Harwich's rise to becoming a world-class, deep-water international port. Already, by the end of the nineteenth century it was Britain's most important passenger port, plying between England, Belgium and the Netherlands.

By 1884, the London, Tilbury & Southend Railway had connected Fenchurch Street Station in London with Grays, Tilbury, Southend and Shoeburyness.

SHOEBURY GARRISON

There had been delay in completing the final stretch of railway between Southend and Shoeburyness, some say due initially to the military's concerns about security. Eventually, the eastern extremity of the line reached Shoebury High Street, at the end of which stood Shoebury Garrison.

The garrison originated in 1849 on a narrow coastal strip of land purchased from a local farmer. The army rented areas of sand and pegged out firing lines, initially to a maximum of 6,000 yards. The first firing battery was constructed that winter and new guns were brought down from Woolwich during the summer months to be tested. Barges sailed from Woolwich to the garrison pier where sheer legs and derricks lifted the heavy guns ashore. These massive weapons fired on to the Maplin Sands and the sea would conveniently withdraw twice a day to enable the fired shells to be collected and studied.

Local fishermen may have grumbled about the inconvenience, but for other local residents, such as gentleman farmer Christopher Parsons, firing days offered an opportunity to bring one's wife down to the sands for the afternoon to be entertained by the proceedings.

The first British School of Gunnery was formed at Shoeburyness in 1859 when more land was purchased. A permanent garrison was established there with brick-built barrack blocks, officers' accommodation, mess and a state-of-the-art military hospital.

Experiments began to move to the New Ranges in North Shoebury and Foulness in 1890 as weapon performance improved and longer ranges were needed. By 1915, the

Shoeburyness clocktower, built 1860–61. It stands at the head of the Horseshoe Barracks in Shoebury Garrison.

War Office owned Havengore Island, New England Island and most of Foulness, plus over 30,000 acres of sands.

The School of Gunnery was replaced by the Coast Artillery School in 1920, which remained in Shoebury until 1940. The Proof and Experimental Establishment here has conducted thousands of experiments over the years with everything from war dogs and warship armour to aircraft and atom bombs.

EDUCATING ESSEX

No schoolmaster could be appointed at Maldon between 1768 and 1810 when the town had temporarily lost its borough charter, and many children, not unusually, went uneducated. The Church of England set up the National Society in 1811 with the aim of establishing a school in every parish of England. When the government conducted a survey of education provision in 1818, Maldon was able to boast three schools: the church-funded infant school (St Mary's), a National Primary School and a British School for Nonconformist children.

Manningtree was fortunate, and reported to the authorities in 1818 that seventy-one boys and thirty-two girls were being educated at the National School and 'the poor are generally possessed of the means of education'. But for most rural parishes, the situation was more commonly like that of Steeple Bumpstead (population 800), where two 'respectable' schools were paid for by parents who could afford it, while 'the poor are desirous of learning to read'.

The vicar of Elsenham (population 392) showed a relaxed attitude to education when he appeared complacent that 'all children of the poor may receive instruction at the Sunday school'. Even Great Burstead (which included the smaller village of Billericay) with a population of 1,533 and seven fee-paying schools reported, 'The poorer classes are without sufficient means of educating their children and are desirous of possessing them'. Brentwood at least had a schoolroom, although part of it was being used as a stable in the 1820s. A school for 300 workhouse children from Shoreditch opened in Brentwood in 1854; one of its masters was imprisoned for cruelty to children in 1894.

At Hallsville, West Ham, the National School was a basic wooden lean-to built at the end of an unfinished terrace of houses. It was put up to accommodate the eleven local children of school age. However, the population grew so rapidly that the shabby hut soon had over 100 children crammed into it. In the winter months, the schoolmistress taught with an umbrella held over her head to deflect the rain which came in through the roof. Luckily for both mistress and pupils, by the mid-1850s a local bowling alley had become available and the school transferred there, although windows were kept tightly shut against the stench rising from the open sewer.

A report of 1867 found that 759 pupils were attending the fourteen remaining endowed grammar schools in Essex, although 585 of those were paying for the privilege. There were nearly 800 other schools in the county (including twelve workhouse schools), with places for 60,000 children. Colchester, West Ham and Halstead were providing Ragged Schools for orphans and the destitute, but forty-two of the smallest Essex parishes had no school at all. This left about 300,000 children in Essex with no education provision.

The situation was worst in the south-west where populations were growing at an ever-increasing rate. The 1870 Education Act demanded Board Schools to be set up where needed, with parishes authorised to raise money locally to pay for them. However, in rural Essex many families were dependent on the pennies their children earned as casual farm labour, and so schooling was not popular.

AGRICULTURAL DEPRESSION

During the 1850s and 1860s, agriculture flourished in Essex and there was a trend towards grubbing up woodland to provide more fields. On the north Essex border, skilled workers could earn 3s 6d per twenty straw plaits, making about thirty plaits a week. Many wives and children in Helions Bumpstead boosted the family income this way. Agricultural labourers' wages averaged 8 or 9s a week, but were 2 or 3s a week lower in north-west Essex. Despite this, a Clavering farmer felt his workers were 'amply provided for' because 6s would buy 'nearly enough bread for a family with five children' and, when a man was unemployed, 'we keep him in the workhouse'.

By contrast, handloom weavers at Braintree and Halstead were earning 12s a week, if they worked fifteen hours a day. At Brightlingsea, Wivenhoe and Colchester about 500 men and 160 boats were engaged in the oyster trade, also earning about 12s a week during the season – August to April. They collected oyster spawn from the Channel Islands and fattened them up in the Colne.

However, between 1870 and 1890 a series of poor harvests in England, along with cheap imports of corn from Canada and America caused a major agricultural depression, and farmers began to feel the pinch as much as their labourers. The vicar at Ramsden Crays even refused to hold a harvest thanksgiving in 1881. Some were pushed to abandon farming altogether. Because of this, Scottish immigrants who arrived with expertise in dairy farming were able to purchase farmland cheaply and did well for themselves. Also, the development of drainage techniques below the surface allowed farmers to cultivate more of the marshland around the fringes of Essex, although livestock grazing remained important.

Lord Rayleigh in Terling also sustained his farm by concentrating on his dairy herds and Isaac Mead of Good Easter specialised in poultry farming, while Arthur

Wilkins of Tiptree modified his fruit farm into a jam factory. Colchester became known for flower growing, sending 100 tons of roses and lilies to London every year. In Foxearth, Reverend John Foster financed a brewery to provide alternative employment for the villagers.

NEW INDUSTRIES AND 'BUBBLING CESSPOOLS'

The ready supply of labour displaced from the fields fed the growth of south-west Essex, where proximity to both the River Thames and London provided an ideal location for new industries and, in particular, the Royal Victoria Dock, which opened in 1855.

Sand and gravel extraction provided opportunities in the Lea Valley, and brickfields flourished in the south-east, where glacial brickearth was widespread. Thames barges were a common sight, transporting agricultural produce, timber, coal and bricks. Bargees also benefited from the need to transport refuse from London, which was used in the brick manufacturing process. The circular brick lime kiln at Beaumont Quay in Tendring is today the only complete lime kiln surviving in Essex. Such kilns were common in the 1800s, usually built near to chalk quarries to be close to the raw materials they needed. Other kilns were built near harbours and wharfs were chalk and coal could be brought in by sea.

Samuel Winkworth Silver's rubber factory opened in 1852, originally making waterproof clothing. The company expanded to become the India Rubber, Gutta Percha and Telegraph Cable Company. It was quickly joined by a number of chemical works and petroleum storage depots. By 1864, the area became its own ecclesiastical parish, named Silvertown.

Henry Tate (in 1877) and Abram Lyle (in 1881) set up separate sugar refining companies in the area and were bitter business rivals. They had no idea that their companies would merge into Tate & Lyle in 1921, after both their deaths.

Dockworkers, warehousemen, carters, builders and packers settled near to the work on marshy land that had previously been thought uninhabitable, throwing up makeshift cottages in a squalid, chaotic morass. There was no water supply or sewerage system, save for the open ditches that the residents dug for themselves.

Arguably, the least healthy area of Essex was Canning Town, named for Charles John Canning, the first Viceroy of India. Charles Dickens visited Canning Town in 1857 and described the ditches as 'a cesspool charged with corruption ... bubbling and seething with the constant rise of the foul products of decomposition'. The walkways between the cottages 'enable men to walk not more than midleg deep' in mud. Dickens' description is vivid. 'We smell the [dead] dog, we smell the ditches, and we smell the marsh,' he said.

A doctor in the 1850s reported regular epidemics of fever and smallpox, while the vicar recorded sixteen deaths in Plaistow but seventy-two in Hallsville over the same time period. In fact, many parish registers for the first half of the nineteenth century record deaths due to symptoms similar to tuberculosis and dysentery, as well as cholera and typhoid, indicating that much of Essex was far from a healthy environment.

In Chelmsford, the sale of the Mildmay estate in the 1840s created a building boom that saw the construction of many grand houses on what is now New London Road, and on the land on both sides. This exacerbated the already unacceptable situation concerning the disposal of sewage, and when cholera broke out, there was impetus to address 'the very filthy and unwholesome state of several of the drains and ditches' which discharged into the rivers.

In September 1850, five families living in Leigh High Street each lost a baby. They blamed the local witch, Sarah Moore, but a more likely cause is the filthy water from the village pump. Similar situations all over the country eventually led to the 1848 Public Health Act and the formation of local Boards of Health in the most densely populated areas. These bodies were given powers to control sewers, clean the streets, regulate environmental health risks, such as slaughterhouses, and ensure the proper supply of water to their districts.

COMMUNITY LEADERS

Victorian towns and villages were keen to benefit from modern piped water supplies, electric lighting and education but often lacked the finances to bring these facilities to their localities. In many cases, leading citizens became town benefactors by spending their own time and money to benefit their communities.

In Saffron Walden, the Quaker Gibson family made their money in malting, brewing and banking. They were instrumental in founding the Friends School, the British School, the hospital, gasworks and the new water company. The Gibson Garden is still enjoyed by the public today.

James Gigney took over his father's ironmongery in the 1870s and became one of the first parish councillors in Wickford. He was active in improving the lighting and water supplies to the village. Farmer Henry Smith built a town hall for Great Bardfield and paid for a horse-drawn manual fire engine. In Southend, jeweller Robert Jones, like Gibson, was a believer in public open spaces and gave the town three large public parks.

EARTHQUAKE: 'CHILDREN TIPPED FROM BENCHES'

An earthquake, the strongest ever felt in Britain (an estimated 5.2 on the Richter scale), rocked Essex in 1884.
Although the vibrations were estimated to have lasted no
more than ten seconds, over 1,000 buildings in east Essex
suffered damage on that Tuesday morning, 22 April. The
Essex Field Club compiled a comprehensive study of the
effects of the earthquake, providing a snapshot of its effects.

At Rochford, 'a man in a shoemaker's shop rushed out of
doors with his shoe off, thinking the shop was about to fall
in'. At Ramsey vicarage, a 'servant in the upper storey had
to lay hold of the bedstead to prevent herself from being
thrown down', and at Mountnessing, 'oscillation [was] felt
by a person in bed'. Mr W. Aberdein helpfully compared
the sound accompanying the shock to 'the discharge of a
68-pound gun on the upper deck as felt in the lower deck
of a ship'.

The worst effects of the quake were seen in north-east
Essex, for example at Colchester (414 damaged buildings), in Wivenhoe (259 damaged buildings) and East
Donyland (207 damaged buildings). In Colchester High
Street, as elsewhere, many chimney stacks were 'thrown
down'. The church bells began to ring themselves and at
St Mary's School, Colchester, 'some little children were
tipped from their benches'. Cracks appeared in several
church towers.

Wivenhoe was one of the worst hit areas and shopkeeper
Mr Stebbing reported, 'Tins of lobster and salmon rolled
about the shop by scores; things were tumbling down in all
directions ... I thought I would be buried alive.' However,
there were no serious injuries here or elsewhere.

At Peldon, some villagers could not live in their homes
until repairs had been completed. The church was severely
damaged and the Rose Inn lost part of its roof. Many places,
such as Abberton, Brightlingsea, Layer Breton, Langenhoe,

Rowhedge and West Mersea, lost most of their chimneys, while Layer Marney Tower suffered considerable damage and required expensive renovations.

Previous earthquakes were recorded as affecting Essex in 1247, in 1692 'along the Thames', and in 1750 in west Essex.

The Kings Head, Chigwell, built in 1547 and described by Charles Dickens as 'a delicious old inn' in an 'out-of-the-way rural place'.

ESSEX COUNTY COUNCIL, 1889

Parliament created county councils in England in 1889 and Essex County Council was based in Chelmsford, although it met in London until 1938. Three of the most densely populated areas – West Ham, East Ham and Southend-on-Sea – successfully applied to become 'municipal boroughs', responsible for their own rates and administration.

The Liberty of Havering became a part of Essex and the last high bailiff was awarded a pension of £3 a year for life, while small parts of Helions Bumpstead and Sturmer became part of Suffolk (including the farm that produced 'Essex apples' – the Sturmer Pippin). Part of Hadstock, Ashdon, Great Horkesley, Chishill and Chrishall joined Cambridgeshire.

In 1894, the county was divided into five municipal boroughs (Chelmsford, Colchester, Maldon, Saffron Walden and Southend-on-Sea), plus urban districts and rural districts.

SCIENCE, INDUSTRY AND INNOVATION: A NOBEL PRIZE FOR ESSEX

The second half of the nineteenth century saw industry flourish in Essex's larger towns, aided by cheap rail transport and a supply of labourers who could no longer find work in agriculture. In Chelmsford, for example, Christy Brothers established their engineering firm in 1858, followed by Colonel Crompton's electrical engineering company in 1880 and Hoffmann's ball-bearing company in 1898. Hoffman's achieved worldwide fame for precision-made bearings and their products were used in the first transatlantic flights. For many years, Hoffman's was Chelmsford's main employer.

John William Strutt was born in Maldon in 1842. He inherited the title 3rd Baron Rayleigh in 1873 and moved into Terling Place with his wife Eleanor Balfour (whose brother later became the prime minister). John experimented with electromagnetism and acoustics and was the first person to be able to explain why the sky looks blue – a scattering of particles, still known as the 'Rayleigh effect'. His most significant discovery was of the colourless, odourless element argon, for which he received a Nobel Prize. He became president of the Royal Society and continued scientific research until his death in 1919.

PHILANTHROPISTS

Young William Morris (1834–96), who was born in Walthamstow, liked nothing better than to roam the ancient forests admiring the patterns and shapes of the trees and leaves. He grew up to be one of Britain's most well-known and best-loved designers of fabric, furniture and wallpaper, using nature's designs in his work.

William became a founding member of the Society for the Protection of Ancient Buildings. In 1884, he formed the Socialist League and later helped to found the Hammersmith Socialist Society. He advocated fair wages for all classes of people and believed that everyone should have access to beauty in their own homes.

William Booth (1829–1912) had been working with the unemployed and homeless in London for years, eventually founding the Salvation Army. He saw a need for training facilities that could not be provided in an urban environment. In 1891, he took the railway into Essex and purchased 800 acres of farmland at Hadleigh, later extending this to over 3,000 acres. His vision, titled the 'Darkest England Project' was to provide employment, food and lodgings in return for labour to 'any man who is willing to work, irrespective of nationality or creed'. The Hadleigh colony trained thousands of men in agriculture, setting them up for independent living, and many of the younger men were sent to Australia or Canada to make a new life for themselves.

Irishman Dr Thomas Barnardo (1845–1905) began working with homeless boys in the East End in 1870. Five years later, he laid the foundation stones for a village for orphaned girls at Barkingside and officially opened the first thirteen cottages in July 1876. The girls were trained in baking, laundry work and needlework and most of them went into domestic service, often in Canada or Australia. The village finally closed in 1991 and much of the site was redeveloped, although a few features, such as the entrance gates, have been retained for posterity.

8

A NEW CENTURY: WORK AND PLAY

The 1901 census discovered that the population of Essex had increased by 38.2 per cent since 1891. This was a greater increase than in any other county in the United Kingdom (the average rate of increase for the UK was just under 10 per cent). This spectacular growth was explained by Essex's proximity to London, although Kent had only increased by 18 per cent over the same period and Surrey by 16 per cent. The population of Walthamstow had more than doubled, and that of East Ham almost trebled in ten years.

Between 1891 and 1911, Leyton's population grew from 63,000 to 125,000 and Ilford's grew from 11,000 to 78,000. The birth rate was not unusually high, but a significant percentage of inhabitants had been born in London, showing that people were moving into the area. By 1900, housing development in the most populous districts, West Ham, East Ham and Walthamstow, joined these areas to London.

By 1914, more than half the population of Essex (some 700,000 people) were living in less than 10 per cent of the county's area. Southend-on-Sea became a county borough in 1914, closely followed by East Ham (1915–65). The new diocese of Chelmsford was created in 1914 and the Church of St Mary became Chelmsford Cathedral (dedications to St Peter and St Cedd were added in the 1950s). The population of Colchester had reached 38,000.

Almshouses at Little Easton built by Banastre Lord Maynard about 1716 for the residence of four poor widows.

EDWARD VII AND ESSEX

Two days before Edward Prince of Wales was due to be crowned as Edward VII, his doctor called upon the 'most eminent surgeons in the land' to advise on his stomach pains. One of these respected medical professionals was Joseph Lister, who had been born in Upton, Essex, in 1827. Joseph recommended immediate surgery for appendicitis and the coronation was postponed for six weeks.

Joseph was the first to realise and practise the benefits of antiseptic when performing medical operations. His experiments with carbolic acid in 1865 cut the death rate of his patients from 45 per cent to 15 per cent. Later, he became surgeon to Queen Victoria when she was in Scotland.

Thirty years before his coronation, the prince had consulted another Essex-born doctor, William Withy Gull, about an attack of typhoid fever. William Gull had been born on a barge at the Hythe, Colchester, and left fatherless at 11, but rose to become a highly respected doctor. He conducted ground-breaking research into Bright's disease and Anorexia Nervosa, which he named. Speculation that William might have had a double life as Jack the Ripper is unfounded.

But Prince Edward had had closer links with Essex than through his doctors. In 1889, he met the beautiful Frances Greville, Countess of Warwick, and began a nine-year affair, calling her 'my darling Daisy'. Together they danced, socialised and partied, often at Daisy's family home Easton Lodge, near Great Dunmow. Later, Daisy became a Socialist and helped the local poor with, among other schemes, a sewing school at Little Easton to train girls for employment.

Coronation day finally arrived on 9 August 1902, once the prince had recovered from his operation. The weavers of Braintree listened for reports with more interest than most as they had personally woven the cloth that made the coronation robes, including a gold cloth. Braintree villagers held a procession to mark the occasion. The weavers were drawn along the High Street in a cart with their looms, while the women who had prepared the silk for the weavers rode on a second cart.

Braintree Market, 1826.

Most villages celebrated the coronation by providing a tea for children and the poor. Billericay roasted a whole ox outside the Red Lion Hotel and gave a show of fireworks around a huge bonfire. The bells of Sible Hedingham rang out at intervals throughout the day, while 100 members of the poor received 1s 6d. The children of Hutton enjoyed a ventriloquist and conjuring entertainment after their tea and were each given a commemorative mug. The choir of All Saints, Witham, performed 'Zadoc the Priest' and a committee of ladies at Maldon had made a silk flag depicting the historic borough arms.

SEASIDE HOLIDAYS

Since Princess Caroline's visit in 1804 and Emma Hamilton's ball at its Royal Hotel, Southend had struggled to achieve its ambitions as a high-class holiday resort. A significant reason for this was the lack of good access. The quickest transport was the Thames passenger steamers, but at low tide visitors were faced with the problem of crossing the wide expanse of river mud between ship and shore. Local fishermen earned good money for physically carrying ladies across the ooze, but it was not the most dignified way to arrive!

Locals campaigned for a pier to reach out to ships in the deep-water channel and crowds gathered at the top of Southend's main street to greet local MP William Heygate as he arrived, hotfoot from Parliament, with news on their decision. Everybody cheered and shouted, and William was the hero of the hour when he leaned from his carriage and announced that Southend had permission to build a pier. A committee set to immediately and a wooden pier opened in 1830. It was a wise move and visitor numbers increased rapidly.

When the railway from east London reached central Southend in 1856, a new kind of visitor was attracted to the town. Day trippers and weekend visitors from the East

Mr Southend, from the *Southend and Westcliff Graphic*, 1907, illustrating the expansion of the seaside town.

End and west Essex crammed into the railway carriages and flooded into Southend. The Royal Hotel and elegant terraces built on the west cliff were not for them: they demanded cheap accommodation, public entertainments and kiss-me-quick hats.

Southend Pier was reborn as an iron structure in 1889 and extended in both 1898 and 1929 to become the longest pleasure pier in the world at 1.34 miles long. Further along the seafront, the Kursaal, one of the world's first purpose-built amusement parks, opened in 1901, attracting thousands of visitors each year.

Walton-on-the-Naze built its own pier in 1870. The town was necessarily brand new as most of the original village, including its church, had fallen into the sea during the 1790s and had been washed away with the crumbling cliff on which it was built.

A year later, in 1871, Clacton Pier opened and Peter Schulyer Bruff embarked on developing a new resort, creating a new settlement on the coast distinct from the original village at Great Clacton. He called it 'Clacton-on-Sea'. Many people were tempted to settle in the town permanently and Clacton became an urban district that same year.

At Canvey Island, entrepreneur Frederick Hester envisaged a 'Winter garden' with tropical plants, restaurants and a railway. He began executing his plans around 1900 but was unable to secure financial investment, so his ambitious plans came to nothing.

FOREST VISITORS

The countryside of west Essex was attracting its own visitors. From 1824, they enjoyed walking to Pole Hill to see the granite obelisk newly erected on the Greenwich meridian. Astronomers at the Greenwich Royal Observatory could use the obelisk to set their telescopes to true north as this was the highest point on that bearing directly visible from Greenwich. But, current astronomers beware – an international agreement in 1884 changed the line of 0° longitude to run 19ft *east* of the obelisk.

Government commissioners took over Epping Forest's forest rights in 1851 and sold them, as part of the enclosure process. Within six weeks, over 3,000 acres of Hainault Forest was felled with the idea of releasing land for agriculture or building. By 1865, 4,000 acres of Epping Forest had been enclosed. A colony of ninety-six gypsies lived in Epping Forest in elaborately painted caravans and barrel-shaped tents. They made their living by selling tinware and brooms.

When Chingford Station opened in 1873, Londoners took advantage of weekends in Epping Forest, with beer tents, games, donkey rides and fortune tellers laid on for them. Pubs, clubs and churches organised day trips for their members.

Thomas Willingale was keen to retain his right to take branches from the wood for fuel, and he filed a lawsuit against the lord of the manor of Loughton for enclosing and selling part of the forest. Unfortunately, Thomas died before the case concluded, but he had raised awareness of the loss of the forest.

The Corporation of London purchased 5,531 acres of unenclosed land in the early 1870s and in 1878 secured the Epping Forest Act, which established them as the Conservators of Epping Forest and finally abolished the medieval forest laws. Then, Londoners could continue to enjoy the forest, and loppers like Thomas Willingale were compensated to the tune of £3 11s each, although gypsy camps were banned.

Queen Victoria herself travelled by train to Chingford and formally opened the forest to the public on 6 May 1882, declaring it available 'for the use and enjoyment of my people for all time'. Several tramps took her at her word and took up residence in the wood, giving the forest a reputation for 'hermits'.

Today, the Epping Forest Committee is responsible for managing the area.

CRITTALL WINDOWS

Here comes Frank Crittall (1860–1935) on one of his twice-daily tours of his window frame manufacturing company in Braintree. The workers are happy to see their plump and genial boss as he stops to chat about how the work is going today.

Frank was brought up above his family's ironmonger's in Bank Street, Braintree. He worked a 70-hour week as soon as he was old enough and remembers feeling lucky for a scape of butter on his bread. He took over his father's business in 1883 and eventually began to specialise in metal window frames.

Mindful of his own background, Frank Crittall was the first employer in the world to introduce a five-day working week for his workers, beating Fords of Detroit by a good six months. He even heated his factories. But above Frank's kind heart was an astute business brain. He won contracts to supply windows to Flixton Hall in Suffolk and the House of Commons. He sent his son to forge business links in the United States and opened factories there. Under Frank's benign yet watchful eye, the business grew into an international concern and a world leader in window manufacture.

AN EXPLOSIVES FACTORY

In 1897, George Kynoch opened an explosive factory east of Shell Haven Creek, producing cordite, guncotton, gunpowder and cartridges. The estate built to house employees became known as Kynochtown. The Kynoch works closed in 1919 and the site was taken over by Cory Brothers Ltd for an oil storage depot and Kynochtown was renamed Coryton.

An oil refinery (Vacuum Oil Company, and later Mobil) took over the site in 1950, expanding to absorb the whole of Coryton village by 1970. Operations passed to BP and then Petroplus but the oil refinery closed in May 2012. After lengthy negotiations, the site became a storage depot for diesel in 2016. The site is now named Thames Oilport.

THE WIRELESS TELEGRAPH

When young Guglielmo Marconi applied to the Italian authorities for funding for his research into a wireless telegraph system, he was referred to the lunatic asylum. A friend suggested he might find a more supportive attitude in England, and so Guglielmo, his prototype radio equipment and his English mother arrived in London in 1896.

He began to demonstrate his ideas to anyone who would listen and was able to set up business in Hall Street, Chelmsford, in December 1898 as the Wireless, Telegraph & Signal Co. Ltd. It was the first radio factory in the world. The company moved to new purpose-built premises in New Street, Chelmsford, in 1912, where the two huge 450ft aerial masts became a prominent feature of the town. A few years later, the company took on an additional site in Writtle where they tested voice radio for aircraft.

In 1919, Marconi was given a licence to broadcast test transmissions from New Street. Volunteers read whatever was to hand (for example railway timetables) or sang to test the transmitters but keen radio owners wrote to request more entertaining output. On 15 June 1920, Australian opera singer Dame Nellie Melba arrived at New Street. She alighted from a white Rolls-Royce and strode in, her high leather boots clicking across the polished floor. She stood where she was told, in front of a microphone, and sang. Her voice entertained people across the whole world in this historic event: Britain's first official public entertainment broadcast. The *Daily Mail*, who predicted commercial potential in public entertainment broadcasts, paid Nellie handsomely for her 'appearance'.

The Postmaster General, however, was not amused at this 'trivial' use of radio. He had concerns that it interfered with communications at Croydon Airport and felt so strongly that Marconi's licence to transmit was removed. Dame Nellie was also worried that radio broadcasts might reduce audiences at her live shows and so she never performed on radio again.

Soon, Marconi's 'Hut' at Writtle was licensed for public broadcasts and began Britain's first regular radio broadcasts, every Tuesday evening during 1922. From these modest beginnings, the British Broadcasting Company – the BBC – was formed. Thousands turned out for the state funeral in Rome when Marconi died there in 1937. In Britain, all BBC and Post Office transmitters observed two minutes of silence in his honour.

9

TWO WARS AND A HOUSING CRISIS

THE FIRST WORLD WAR

When war was declared in 1914 the *Chelmsford Chronicle* reported, 'The National Reserves of all the county have been called up and all Wednesday and yesterday they were pouring into the town and presenting themselves at the Territorial Offices'. Chelmsford Cattle Market was opened specifically to deal with horses which had been requisitioned for use in the army. There were 200 men from Hoffman's, 100 from Arc Works and forty from the Steam Car Company, who reported at the army offices, although the workers were officially on their annual holiday.

Three ships, the *Royal Edward*, *Ivernia* and *Saxonia*, arrived at Southend Pier where they detained over 4,000 civilian and military prisoners of war, until May 1915 when alternative accommodation was found.

Barracks in the county were overflowing and soldiers were billeted in tents or in people's houses. Some, like Ellen Willmott of Great Warley, welcomed this as she could charge the army rent on her cottages. Others were not so keen, like William Young of Chelmsford, who complained that soldiers were using 'filthy language' in front of his son.

Harwich became a naval port and a restricted area. Most workhouses became barracks or prisoner-of-war camps. The Dunmow Workhouse served as both, and Romford's workhouse became a military hospital.

ZEPPELIN RAIDS

The first major Zeppelin air raids on Britain targeted Southend and Westcliff on 10 May 1915, when a Zeppelin LZ38 dropped 120 bombs. The damage and the death of Agnes Whitwell led to angry townsfolk attacking shops suspected of having links with Germany. The Reserve Battalion of the Essex Regiment was dispatched to stabilise the situation. The same Zeppelin returned to bomb Southend again on 26 May.

Twelve Zeppelins attacked the east coast on the night of 23–24 September 1916. The L32 crossed the Thames into Essex at Purfleet and was greeted by fire from AA guns at Thurrock and Belhus Park. The Zeppelin dropped thirty-two high-explosive and twenty-seven incendiary bombs between Aveley and South Ockendon, although most fell in open countryside. The AA guns at Tilbury and Fobbing had the airship in their sights but it was Fred Sowrey of 39 Squadron who caused the Zeppelin to burst into flames. It crashed at Great Burstead, killing the crew of twenty-two men.

Zeppelin L33, commanded by Kapitänleutnant Alois Bocker, also crash-landed in Essex. It had crossed Foulness and bombed South Fambridge before dropping six incendiaries on Upminster Common and six high-explosive bombs at South Hornchurch near the airfield. The Zeppelin then killed six people in West Ham, damaged the North London Railway works, a Baptist chapel and the Black Swan pub, where another five people died. It continued dropping bombs over Stratford Marsh, the British Petroleum Company works and Judd's Match Factory, despite being hit by AA fire.

The airship was again hit by AA fire from Kelvedon Common but it reached the coast at Mersea. However, realising they would never make it across the sea, Bocker turned the Zeppelin back and crash-landed at Little Wigborough. The Zeppelin crew of twenty-two allowed themselves to be escorted into custody by Special Constable Edgar Nicholas, who had arrived on his bicycle.

When LZ38 passed over Essex on 31 May 1916, its target was London. Fifteen aircraft were launched to bring it down. Flight Lieutenant Robertson took off from Rochford and followed the Thames, intending to intercept the airship but his engine failed and he crash-landed in the mud at Leigh-on-Sea. Finally, as the airship returned home, the mobile AA detachment at Burnham sent up 179 rounds of 1-pounder ammunition while Southminster fired twenty rounds, both unsuccessfully.

By September 1916, the Germans had developed a new plane, the Gotha, and launched new attacks. These biplanes often approached via Foulness, which was an identifiable landmark, using Epping and Chingford reservoirs as similar navigation aids. Harwich was bombed on 22 July and Southend and Shoeburyness on 12 August 1916, with several lives lost. Harwich was again attacked in January 1917 when a dozen enemy planes killed eleven people and wounded thirty-six more.

AIRFIELDS

South Fambridge had been the site of Britain's first airfield when, in 1909, Mr Pemberton Billings attracted hundreds of enthusiasts to his 'flying colony' – although no planes actually managed to get off the ground.

As a direct result of the Zeppelin and Gotha attacks, the Royal Flying Corps took control of several small airfields across Essex. For example, they acquired Stow Maries Aerodrome in September 1916. The airfield covered 15 acres and had forty-four buildings at its peak. By late 1919 the need for air defence had lowered and the use of the smaller airfields was discontinued. Hornchurch Airfield became operational in October 1915 specifically to defend London. Pilot Lieutenant William Leefe Robinson, operating from Hornchurch, received a Victoria Cross for his war record.

WAR WORK

Of course, businesses had to deliver the new government orders for war goods with many fewer men to work, so Essex girls stepped forward. Annie Overton, for example, volunteered to work on the trams in Southend and became the first female tram driver in the country.

Frank Crittall personally sidled a shell out of the War Office and dissected it at home. He worked out how to put it together, changed all his machinery over to making them, and turned out the first 20,000 in two months. Crittall also negotiated government backing for the formation of the East Anglian Munitions Committee, which enabled small firms to contribute to the production of military equipment. Furthermore, by charging far lower prices for the production of shells, he was able to break the stranglehold of the disgraceful armaments ring with its attitude to profiteering from the war. He also pressed for the appointment of a director to supervise the exploitation of scrap metal and the recovery and reuse of metal from the battlefields.

Samuel Williams & Sons, who had a deep-water jetty at Dagenham, established a fleet of ships to bring coal from Scotland and Tyneside to keep the Thames industries working. The last warship to be launched in the Thames was the Dreadnought *Thunderer*, built by the Thames Ironworks at Canning Town and fitted out at Dagenham Dock.

Tragically, seventy-three people died when the TNT factory exploded at Silvertown in January 1917. There were another 400 severely injured and the immediate area was devastated. Seven months later, the Ajax Chemical Works at Barking, which had been making shells, exploded killing thirteen people.

The Waltham Abbey gunpowder mills were asked to increase production to meet the demands of the war. Their pre-war annual output of 26 tonnes of high explosives was to become 150 tonnes a year. There was no choice but to recruit 3,000 female workers to join the existing staff of 600 men. By the end of the war, 6,200 staff were employed, half of whom were female. While the men took on the skilled work, such as mixing ingredients, the women mucked in with operating the railways and stoking the boiler house fires.

Wilkin & Sons of Tiptree sent 8,000 boxes of jam to the front to boost morale, while Hoffmann's supplied the aircraft industry throughout both great wars.

Over 5,000 members of the Australian and New Zealand Army Corps were stationed at Brightlingsea during the First World War. An Australian Engineers Training Depot was established in Brightlingsea between 1916 and 1919. They trained in bridge, pontoon and road building. They dug trenches and tunnels and trained in front-line military tactics.

LAND GIRLS

Lady Petre and Miss Courtauld launched the Essex Women's War Agricultural Association in March 1916, and Lady Byng chaired an early meeting at Colchester Town Hall. Recruitment rallies were held across the county and, by June, 500 women were already at work on farms and over 3,500 more had volunteered.

At Thorndon Hall, Lady Petre began a school to train children to help out at farms and within a year, over 100 women had also been trained there – they joined the 6,000 women working on the land in Essex by that time.

Six official training centres for female farmworkers were set up around Essex, for example at Layer-de-le-Haye, where women learnt thatching, coppicing and rat catching in addition to general field work. Essex became a 'show county' with regard to the work and the care taken of the girls. At a recruitment drive in Terling, the Honourable

Edward Strutt called upon local women to join the Land Army for their own health and happiness.

Despite such enterprises, food shortages became a reality. Colchester residents could apply for a free allotment to grow their own food. However, demand from allotment holders caused a rise in the price of seed potatoes, which was detrimental to farmers. In addition, low food prices which helped the general population were another blow to farmers.

By 1919, over 1,100 German prisoners of war were working on the land in Essex alongside the Women's Land Army.

WAR DOGS

Lieutenant Colonel Richardson had been interested in using dogs for war work for several years before he was allowed to establish an official British War Dogs School. He chose Shoeburyness as an ideal location in 1917, as the frequent explosions from ongoing weapons testing there would be good experience for the dogs.

At first, Richardson acquired dogs from the Battersea Dogs Home for his school. The animals proved so worthwhile that police forces across the country were instructed to send any strays to Shoeburyness. Eventually, Richardson appealed to the public to donate their pets for the war effort. One lady donor wrote, 'I have given my husband and my sons, and now that he too is required, I give my dog.'

Airedales were particularly reliable as messenger dogs, but dogs of many breeds were sent to France and Belgium, as well as being used as guards and sentries around Britain. So successful was the War Dogs School that it outgrew its Essex home and was relocated to Salisbury Plain in 1918.

A YOUNG WAR HERO

Meanwhile, 16-year-old Jack Cornwell prepared to serve his country on his first official posting to HMS *Chester*. On 31 May 1916, the ship was engaged at the Battle of Jutland. Jack's job was to relay messages from the bridge to his gun position. Before long, his gun position was attacked and the other members of his team were killed. Although severely wounded himself, Jack remained at his post awaiting orders.

After the battle, Jack was taken to Grimsby Hospital but died of his wounds and was buried in Grimsby. A short while later, Jack was awarded the Victoria Cross: the second youngest person to have received it. His body was exhumed and brought to Manor Park, his home town (then part of Essex) for a public funeral. Several memorial hospitals were named in his honour and Scouts can achieve the Jack Cornwell badge for 'Courage and Endurance'.

Herbert Columbine (1893–1918) of Walton-on-the-Naze. He won a Victoria Cross for manning a machine gun under constant fire to allow his colleagues to escape to safety.

THE END OF THE WAR

At the end of the war, it was agreed that all German submarines would surrender to Admiral Tyrwhitt at Harwich. The first convoy of U-boats with a German transport ship and their crews arrived at the harbour on 20 November and lined up along the Stour. The German crews transferred to the transport ship for the voyage home. The remaining U-boats continued to surrender in batches. By 1 December 1918, 122 had been handed over and were eventually sold off for scrap.

When the Armistice was declared, people took to the streets all over Essex, cheering and waving flags. As part of the celebrations, the Fleet arrived off Southend and anchored there as an exuberant spectacle. During the day, flags waved from the rigging; at night, the ships were lit up.

After the war, the Ministry of Health took over many of the workhouses as hospitals (such as at Billericay, Chelmsford, Rochford and Saffron Walden); some were sold for development (Dunmow and Ongar, for example); others, such as the Halstead one, fell into disrepair and were demolished. The Colchester Workhouse became St Mary's Hospital but that, in turn, closed in 1993 and the site was sold for development.

HOUSING BETWEEN THE WARS

Accommodation was at the forefront of many minds after the First World War. The Essex County Council Housing Committee reported that 2,170 new homes were needed in the county but that 1,982 existing cottages were already condemned and needed to be demolished. *The Times* suggested that 167,911 people in Poplar, Stepney and West Ham, many of them dock workers, were still living in overcrowded conditions.

Canning Town had been badly damaged by wartime bombs. The council drew up plans for a complete rebuild of the area, to reduce population density and add community facilities. The Keir Hardie Estate, for example, included a school and clinic. Several of the old estates, such as Gidea Hall and Hare Hall, were sold off to provide both money for the landowners and housing for the working classes, but unfortunately the homes built here were beyond the reach of the lowest paid.

Therefore, an estate was planned for Becontree at Dagenham. By 1935, 100,000 people lived in 27,000 houses built there; it was the largest public housing development in the world, covering 4 square miles. The intended residents were men returning from the war as well as those bombed out of the East End. For many of the latter, it was their first experience of indoor toilets, running water and private gardens.

The council were keen to maintain standards and drew up a handbook for the residents. Rules included keeping gardens tidy, 'bordered edging and concrete paths do not give the restful effect of turf with neatly trimmed edges'. Council officials patrolled the estate and challenged resi-

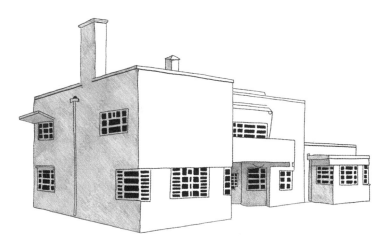

Daniel Crittall's house, Silver End, part of Frank Crittall's vision for workers' housing, built 1926–32.

dents over garden fencing or planting that was not thought to be up to standard.

Meanwhile, in Braintree, Frank Crittall conceived the idea of building a model village for his workforce, who had outgrown his existing factories in Braintree, Maldon and Witham. In the 1920s, he bought the land at Silver End and built a modern village around a new factory. The village comprised designer art deco homes for all, with parks and public halls set in wide, green avenues. Some of the first residents were disabled ex-servicemen who Frank was particularly keen to employ in his factories. Frank himself moved into one of the houses, called 'Manors'.

Similarly, the Bata Shoe Company built not only housing but educational and recreational facilities for their workers, and a real community grew around the factory. The company had been founded by Tomas Bata in Czechoslovakia and had opened a factory in the Essex Marshes at East Tilbury in 1933. Over the following decades the company grew and eventually operated 300 shops across Britain and employed 3,000 people.

The Bata Hotel, part of Bata Shoe Estate, East Tilbury.

PLOTLANDERS AND HOLIDAYMAKERS

An increase of office and factory-based jobs coupled with the increased mechanisation of agriculture was a major reason for a demand for property between the wars. Furthermore, people who had been bombed out of London were looking for opportunities to settle outside the city. The phenomenon of 'plotlands' created opportunities for home ownership and was particularly successful in south-east Essex.

Frank Steadman purchased a plot of land on the coast at Jaywick Sands in 1928 and developed it as a holiday destination for Londoners. Several families decided to settle there permanently. Canvey Island was another popular location, but the largest plotland settlement was at Langdon Hills, Laindon, where new homes included converted railway carriages, buses and redundant army huts.

People who have written reminiscences of plotland life seem to have nothing but happy memories, involving fresh air, homegrown vegetables, bucket toilets, muddy paths and friendly neighbours. However, Dennis Hardy and Colin Ward have described it as a 'makeshift world of shacks and shanties, scattered unevenly'.

Billy Butlin purchased the West Clacton Amusement Park in 1936, built a fun fair there in 1937 and opened a holiday camp the following year. That same year, the government passed the Holidays with Pay Act, which guaranteed all industrial workers at least one week's paid holiday each year. Butlin, with his finger on the pulse, came up with a slogan for his new camp, 'Holidays with pay. Holidays with play! A week's holiday for a week's pay.' The cost of the week was £3 10s – an average wage at the time.

During the Second World War, the camp was requisitioned and used as a training site, although the expected prisoners of war never arrived. Butlin's reopened to the public in 1946. The entertainers included Roy Hudd, Des O'Connor and a young man named Cliff Richard, who made his first professional appearance at Clacton in 1958. The camp remained open until 1983, but eventually, the site was developed as a housing estate.

Weekend sailors now began to holiday at Burnham-on-Crouch and Burnham's Grade II listed Royal Corinthian Yacht Club was designed by Joseph Emberton in 1931, inspired by the International Exhibition of Modern Architecture.

FORD AT DAGENHAM

In the same way that the Industrial Revolution has had a gentler impact on Essex than in northern England, the depression years of the 1920s and 1930s were also less devastating in Essex. Partly, this was due to new businesses attracted by Essex's convenient location to the River Thames, London and the continent.

On 17 May 1929, Edsel Ford, son of Henry, thrust a spade into the Essex marshland at Dagenham as a symbolic gesture of intent to establish the company there. He struck a large stone and the spade bent. This inauspicious beginning did not deter the company and the first vehicle produced on the site rolled off the assembly line in October 1931. It was a model AA truck.

Two thousand employees and their families relocated from the Ford plant in Manchester to start a new life in Essex. Ford gradually expanded to cover around 475 acres and became a global centre of excellence for diesel engineering.

During the Second World War, the Ford factory met the demand for 360,000 military vehicles, including vans, army trucks, mobile canteens and Bren gun carriers.

THE SECOND WORLD WAR

DUNKIRK, JUNE 1940

In early June 1940, British and Allied troops were trapped on the Dunkirk beaches with no means of escape. The authorities appealed for boat owners to come forward, and soon a flotilla of over 700 'little ships' had gathered and their crews had been briefed.

On 6 June, fishermen drinking in the pubs of Leigh-on-Sea were interrupted by an urgent call for all boats to meet at Southend Pier. Dozens of small boats, commercial and private, were soon moored at the pier head. Among them were six cockle bawleys from Leigh. Their owners, skilled and experienced seamen, refused to hand over the boats to the navy – they chose to pilot their own boats instead. Each was assigned a sailor to accompany them.

The small boats set off across the Channel and immediately began to pull men from the sea and ferry them out to the larger ships which could not get into the shore. Back and forth, each boat worked tirelessly all day and through the night. Between them, the ships evacuated 338,266 British and Allied soldiers from Dunkirk.

On the return journey, the fishing boat *The Renown* developed engine trouble and the crew of the *Letitia* threw them a tow line. A few hours later, the exhausted crew of *Letitia* was awoken by an almighty explosion and a shower of wooden splinters. *The Renown* had hit a sea mine, destroying the boat and all on board.

Sixteen Thames barges were also part of the Dunkirk fleet. The *Ena* had been built at Harwich in 1906. Under constant air attack at Dunkirk, *Ena*'s skipper and crew were ordered to abandon ship and escape on a minesweeper. Shortly afterwards, the men of the 19th Field Regiment Royal Artillery arrived on the beach to find a seaworthy barge at their disposal. They got her afloat and eventually arrived at Margate. Meanwhile, Alfred Page, *Ena*'s skipper, had made it back to Ipswich and was amazed to receive a message asking what he was going to do about his barge, which was now moored off Deal.

GHQ LINE

The emergency evacuation from Dunkirk highlighted the urgent need to build defences against the threat of Nazi invasion. The result was the construction of stop-lines: continuous lines of anti-tank obstacles, consisting of man-made objects located to enhance the natural 'lay of the land'.

The General Headquarters Defensive Line was part of this network of defences and crossed Essex with a line of banks, ditches and concrete pillboxes. Over 100 FW3-type pillboxes were built on a line between Great Chesterford and Canvey Island. Dozens more lined the Chelmer Valley between Chelmsford and Great Dunmow. On the seawall, a unique 'Essex Lozenge' pillbox allowed fire in both directions so that enemy troops who had penetrated inland could not pass by.

The Essex coast became out of bounds for the general public. In fact, in 1939 an exclusion zone was identified reaching 25 miles inland. No one was allowed to travel east of London without an official pass. Essex residents travelling between London and their homes had to show their papers. Checkpoints were manned by the police and all stations on both the Southend Liverpool Street and Southend Fenchurch Street rail lines had a policeman permanently on duty.

The exclusion zone was reduced to a 10-mile limit in 1941 and the checkpoints repositioned to the A13 at Bowers Gifford, Pound Lane on the A127, and at the Carpenters Arms on the A129. The Outer London Defence Line followed the River Colne through Nazeing, then ran south through Epping Forest, Loughton and Chigwell. Ditches and anti-tank traps accompanied the pillboxes.

EVACUATION

An advice leaflet produced by the Lord Privy Seal's Office in July 1939 informed the population that 'the "evacuable" areas under the government scheme are: London including West Ham, East Ham, Walthamstow, Leyton, Ilford and Barking in Essex.'

Pat Norris from Stratford spent the first six months of the war at East Mersea before the invasion threat saw her taken back to London where her (unoccupied) school received a direct hit. In June 1940, the decision was later taken to evacuate all children living within 10 miles of the coast, and early one morning schoolchildren lined up at railway stations in Essex coastal towns carrying a small bag and a gas mask each. They had no idea where they were going or when they would see their families again. Children and expectant mothers were evacuated from Grays via a pleasure steamer from Tilbury, around the coast to Lowestoft. Children from Southend and Rochford found themselves in Derbyshire, those from Clacton were sent to Worcestershire while others from Harwich ended up in Gloucestershire.

In September 1940, notices were circulated in Colchester that all old, infirm or retired people, plus women with their children should leave immediately. The thinking was that if everyone who did not need to remain in the town for their work moved out, it would be easier for the army to operate.

When no air raids had occurred for some months, several Essex evacuees began to return home. Schools which had been completely closed reopened, at least for part of the day. Once air raid shelters had been built, the schools returned to full-day teaching, often interrupted by spells of sitting in the shelters.

AIRFIELDS FAR AND WIDE

During the Second World War Essex boasted twenty-three airbases. The largest were at North Weald, Hornchurch and Debden, supported by Rochford and Stapleford. All made important contributions to the Battle of Britain.

Easton Lodge Deer Park lost over 10,000 trees to make way for an American airfield there, and by September 1944 there were 2,700 airmen and sixty-eight aircraft stationed at Great Dunmow.

The Boreham Airfield yielded unexpected surprises when it was constructed. Local people suffered a series of misfortunes and mishaps after a large boulder was removed from the new airfield. The explanation was that they had disturbed a witch, whose grave the rock had marked.

Bradwell Bay was adopted by the RAF as a site for damaged aircraft to land on their return from raids on the enemy. It was enlarged into a full airfield in 1941 and, at its height, over 2,000 service personnel were stationed there.

The ground crew of the 381st Bomb Group alighted from the train at Great Yeldham in June 1943. They were the advance party, arriving to establish a base for the group and their B-17 Flying Fortresses at Ridgewell Airfield. It became their home for the next two years.

The RAF's 617 Squadron, the Dam Busters, used the Abberton Reservoir for practice runs for the bombing of German dams in the Ruhr. Wing Commander Guy Gibson, the leader of the raids, referred to it as 'Colchester lake' in his autobiography.

Land was requisitioned at Kelvedon for an RAF ROTOR station. After the war, it became a Regional Government Headquarters and, in the 1960s, a civil defence centre. It is now known as the Kelvedon Secret Nuclear Bunker.

RAF Canewdon, built in 1936, played an important role as part of the Chain Home Defences. These stations detected enemy aircraft at sufficient distances from the coast for fighter planes to be scrambled to intercept the bombers before they reached their targets.

Between September 1944 and March 1945, Essex shared the brunt of the V-2 missile attacks with London, with much loss of life.

ATTACKS ON INDUSTRY

EKCO, Eric Cole's radio company, began making wirelesses for the army and adapted their Bakelite presses to munitions work, but production was moved away from Southend during the war as industries were an obvious target for enemy bombs. Explosive production was moved from Waltham Abbey to the West Country and the Essex site became a research centre after the war, finally closing in 1991.

On the first night of the Blitz, Tate & Lyle's sugar refinery, John Knight's Primrose Slopworks and the Silvertown Rubber Works were all badly damaged by bombing. Similarly, seventeen of the 6,000 people who worked for Marconi's during the war died when the Chelmsford factory was bombed in 1941.

In August 1942, the Luftwaffe dropped three 500lb bombs on the west wing of Severalls Psychiatric Hospital. Thirty-eight patients were killed, and a 21-year-old nurse, Muriel Jackson, received special praise for her part in rescuing the injured.

The Hoffman Bearings factory, another key target, was attacked on several occasions. The worst single loss of life took place on 19 December 1944 when a V-2 rocket fell on Henry Road near the factory. Thirty-nine people were killed and 138 injured.

10

MODERN TIMES

NEW TOWNS: HARLOW AND BASILDON

After the war, like the first time around, bombed-out
Londoners needed new homes. Furthermore, increasing
wages and improved transport links encouraged them to
seek a better standard of living for their families, away from
the city. The 1946 New Towns Act provided for extensive
new housing, such as the great housing estates at Belhus,
in Aveley and South Ockendon, built by the London
County Council.

The minister for town and country planning met local
representatives in July 1946 to discuss proposals for a
new town based around the little village of Harlow. Essex
County Council then commissioned a young architect,
Frederick Gibberd, to design 'a New Town for post-war
Britain'. Its claim to fame was the first high-rise residential
tower block, The Lawn, and the first all-pedestrian shopping precinct. Gibberd himself settled in a home on the
outskirts of the town.

The people of Laindon gathered at a similar public
enquiry in October 1948. Subsequently, the government
designated 7,834 acres of land in Billericay and Thurrock

urban districts, centred on the tiny village of Basildon as the site for a new town. Building work began in 1949.

On 18 June 1951, John and Betty Walker walked up the garden path of 61 Redgrave Road to become the first new residents of Basildon. That same day, Eric and Marjorie Hawkridge moved into No. 63. Eric remembers, 'We had hot running water in the bathroom ... but we had a job finding £1 12s 4d a week for the rent'. Stan and Phyllis Martin who moved into No. 59 said, 'It was like moving into paradise'.

Expansion of Basildon continued and by March 1964, nearly 12,000 homes had been built, arranged in ten neighbourhoods. Employment opportunities for the residents improved when Ford transferred their Dagenham tractor operation to Basildon, and then opened a research and engineering centre at Dunton. Cosmetic giant Yardley also moved to Basildon.

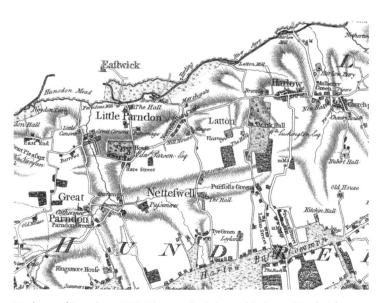

Harlow and Parndon, 1777. The area had changed little until Frederick Gibberd's designs for a new town obliterated the hamlets in 1947.

THE 1953 FLOODS

On the evening of Saturday, 31 January, a north-west wind pushed an unusually full spring tide to an enormous height. The water squeezed down the North Sea where it flooded across the east coast of Britain and the west coast of the Netherlands, in some places to a distance of almost 2 miles inland. This tidal surge locally exceeded 5.6m (18.4ft) above mean sea level defences.

The sea broke into 12,356 Essex homes that night and over 119 people in Essex died, while 21,000 were made homeless. Ray Howard was 10 when the floods hit and recalls the trauma of 'going back to school and seeing which of your classmates hadn't made it'.

On Canvey, many people were woken by water lapping at their beds and dozens were rescued from their roofs by small crafts. Others, like 84-year-old Miss Fowler and her 82-year-old brother, were trapped in their bungalow for days before rescue came. Baby Linda's mother wrapped her carefully in her blanket and Linda floated to safety in her pram while her parents were among the fifty-eight people who lost their lives on Canvey that night.

Others perished from exposure on the roofs of their makeshift Nissen hut homes on Great Wakering Common. Nearby, Foulness Island had disappeared beneath the water and two women and a policeman died there. Thirty-seven people died in Jaywick, where the sea rose a metre in fifteen minutes. The town was completely cut off by the surging water and the police constable risked his life by crawling along the seawall to alert the authorities.

As the water pushed towards London, the banks of the River Thames were breached the length of the Essex coast. From Tilbury to London's docklands, oil refineries, factories, cement works, gasworks and electricity generating stations were flooded and brought to a standstill. All along the east coast, telephone lines were down.

Following the disaster, civilians and servicemen co-operated to repair the sea walls. Services on the flooded railway were not fully restored for almost three weeks. Eventually, the Thames Barrier was completed and Britain developed a scientific coastal flood warning system. In 2013 a service attended by Princess Anne was held at Chelmsford Cathedral to mark the sixtieth anniversary of the 'Great Flood'.

WELCOMING A NEW QUEEN IN 1953

Braintree weavers again had a vested interest in a coronation when they were asked to weave a train for this special occasion in 1953. Immediately following the ceremony, the new Queen Elizabeth donned the exquisite Robe of Purple Velvet before leaving Westminster Abbey. Like the Robe of State, this 6-yard train was made by Ede & Ravenscroft and woven at Warner's of Braintree.

BRADWELL NUCLEAR POWER STATION

The UK government embarked on a plan for nuclear power in 1957, and 30 hectares on the Essex coast at Bradwell-on-Sea was one of the chosen locations. The power station began operating in 1962, using two Magnox (magnesium–aluminium alloy) reactors. The station had the potential to output 300 megawatts of electricity and during the 1960s (on a good day) it was supplying enough energy to meet the needs of a population the size of Chelmsford, Colchester and Southend put together.

Bradwell continued to produce electricity until 2002 when a planned process of decommissioning began. It had contributed 60 terawatt-hours of electricity to the National Grid over its lifetime. In October 2015, the UK government signed a deal with the China General Nuclear Power Group and the French company, EDF, to construct a new nuclear power plant on the same site at Bradwell. These companies are now finalising their reactor design and if planning permission is granted, construction could start on the site by 2022.

MODS AND ROCKERS

Groups of 'Mods' dressed in parka jackets and riding Lambretta scooters clashed with rival 'Rockers', character-ised by motorbikes and leathers, at Clacton over the Easter weekend in 1964. Newspapers reported that they had been 'roaring' and 'rampaging' in an 'orgy of hooliganism'. Alan Jones from Dagenham remembers, 'We knew we were going down there for a rumble ... I took on about three or four mods and I got a deck-chair over my head.' Similar gangs made a habit of visiting Southend on bank holidays or weekends and became an icon of the 1960s Essex seaside.

THE UNIVERSITY OF ESSEX

The University Grants Committee approved the application to establish a university in Essex in 1962. Essex County Council donated a 200-acre site at Wivenhoe Park and the first students arrived in 1964. Lord Butler of Saffron Walden was the first chancellor and Sir Albert Sloman was vice chancellor. The teaching and research buildings and six residential tower blocks were gradually built during the 1960s.

ESSEX IN LONDON

1965 BOUNDARY CHANGES
With London overspill swelling the population of west Essex, it was eventually thought that those boroughs on the

Essex border had more in common with the capital than with the county. Therefore, an Act of 1963 abolished the Essex boroughs of West Ham and East Ham and transferred them to Greater London, to form the new London Borough of Newham.

Similarly, Ilford, Wanstead and Woodford, along with part of Chigwell urban district also became part of Greater London as the new London Borough of Redbridge. Romford and Hornchurch became the London Borough of Havering, while Leyton, Chingford and Walthamstow became the London Borough of Waltham Forest. Finally, Barking and Dagenham were combined to make the London Borough of Barking and Dagenham.

BOUNDARY CHANGES POST-1970
In 1972, Essex County Council replaced a stagnant plotland area at South Woodham Ferrers with a modern new town. They purchased land, sweeping away former plotland bungalows, laid out new roads and built a school and shopping and business areas. On 1 April 1974, under the provisions of the Local Government Act 1972, the title of Sheriff of Essex was retitled High Sheriff of Essex. District boundaries were re-examined and the county boroughs lost their independence.

Having been included in statistics for the south-east region for decades, the government decided to count Essex as part of the East of England from 1994. Then, in 1998, Southend-on-Sea and Thurrock achieved unitary authority status, thereby taking over control of their own local services independently of Essex County Council. However, Essex Police covers both the administrative county and the two unitary authorities.

Twelve district and borough councils now exist under the control of the county council: Basildon, Braintree, Brentwood, Castle Point, Chelmsford, Colchester, Epping Forest, Harlow, Maldon, Rochford, Tendring and Uttlesford.

CONNECTING TO THE WORLD

The three Roman roads which first opened Essex up to travellers are now all but obliterated beneath the busy A12, A120, A13, A130, A414 and A127. Two motorways, the M11 and the M25, also now pass through Essex. Emperor Claudius, if he returned today, would be able to cross the Thames with his marauding elephants to Thurrock via the Dartford Tunnel, which opened in 1963, with the second tunnel opened in 1980. They could return via the Queen Elizabeth II Bridge, which opened in 1991 to accommodate the demand from over 130,000 vehicles a day crossing the Thames at this point.

During the 1960s, Southend was London's third busiest airport but that role passed to Stansted in the 1970s. Southend Airport now handles scheduled passenger, charter and business flights, cargo flights, pilot training and recreational flying.

Stansted Airport started life in 1942 as a USAAF bomber base. The British Airports Authority developed the terminal

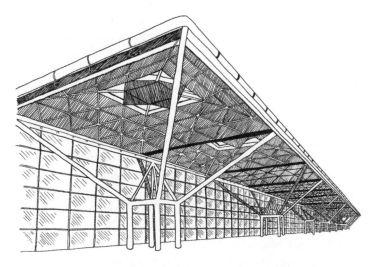

Stanstead Airport, which has won design awards for its architecture.

in 1969 and extended it in 1972. In 1984 it gained approval for expansion and in 1986 work began on the main terminal that stands today. Stansted won numerous awards for the architecture and practicality of the new terminal, opened in 1991. It is now the fourth busiest airport in the United Kingdom. Planes from Stansted fly to over 140 destinations covering thirty-four countries across the world. It was acquired by Manchester Airports Group in 2013 for £1.5 billion and hopes to expand even further.

Harwich International Port has retained its close ties with Europe, while Tilbury is now London's major port.

A NEW MILLENNIUM

Chelmsford welcomed the year 2000 with a spectacular firework and laser show, focused on the cathedral. It was granted a royal charter on 1 June 2012 in celebration of Queen Elizabeth II's Diamond Jubilee and became a city.

The 2012 Olympics were centred on the former Essex town of Stratford, and events were held in the Lee Valley and at Hadleigh Country Park.

Today, Essex appears to be a divided county. It is one of the largest and most densely populated counties in England with thousands of residents commuting to office jobs, many in London. Conversely, 75 per cent of the county has agriculture as the major land use, with winter wheat the main crop. There is also an east–west divide: Jaywick on the east coast has been identified as the most deprived area of England, while Ingatestone and Brentwood are among the twenty wealthiest towns in the UK.

Harlow is a centre for science and pharmaceutical industries, while Chelmsford has been an important location for electronics and financial service companies. Southend has recently lost financial and government employments but is still growing as a regional shopping centre and seaside resort. Its Adventure Island theme park is one of the most popular in Britain. West Thurrock is now one of the largest cement producing areas in Europe. Ferro-alloys are made at Rainham; oil and petroleum are stored at Purfleet in West Thurrock and Grays.

Lakeside Shopping Centre, Thurrock (opened in 1990), is one of the largest shopping centres on one site in Europe. The complex includes over 250 shops, fifty cafes and restaurants and welcomes over 500,000 visitors each week.

Even Frinton, former holiday destination of Hollywood stars, British royalty and politicians, is engaging with the twenty-first century and in 2000 opened its first ever pub 'inside the gates' (south of the railway line).

Colchester Zoo has won several awards for its enclosure development, animal welfare, conservation and breeding programmes. Kito, an African elephant born in 2002, and Zamba, a white rhino born in 2009, were both the first in the world to be conceived by artificial insemination.

Today, there are over 14,000 listed structures in the county. In the north, the Dedham Vale is an Area of Outstanding Natural Beauty, with nationally important scenery (partly thanks to John Constable's paintings). In the south, Southend's 7 miles of foreshore is England's largest wetland nature reserve. In the west, the London fringes retain some of the country's most ancient forests, and in the east, Mersea Island is one of the very few remaining homes of the red squirrel in England.

The Abberton Reservoir is the fourth largest in England with an area of 1,200 acres and is a Site of Special Scientific Interest. Historic grazing marshes around the coast are of international importance for the wintering waterfowl they support, including dark-bellied brent geese and black-tailed godwit, with 2,340 hectares designated as a Special Protection Area.

ESSEX IN THE EU REFERENDUM

In the referendum held in June 2016, when the public were asked to vote on whether to leave the European Union, every district in Essex achieved a higher vote for 'leave' rather than 'remain'. In fact, two of the country's top five 'leave' districts were in Essex: Thurrock (72.3 per cent) and Castle Point (72 per cent). Uttlesford had the highest 'remain' vote in Essex, with 49 per cent. At the time of the vote, Essex had the country's only UKIP MP (Douglas Carswell of Clacton) and sixteen UKIP councillors on Tendring Council.

CONCLUSION

From the Battle of Ashingdon, signing Magna Carta, the Peasants' Revolt, religious dissent, the Civil War, Victorian innovations to the EU referendum, Essex has never been shy of going against the grain and standing up for its beliefs. Its people have invariably been at the forefront of this nation's history. What *will* we do next?

BIBLIOGRAPHY

Banks, Charles Edward, *The Winthrop Fleet of 1630* (reprint Genealogical Publishing, 2003).

Bayne-Powell, Rosamond, *Travellers in Eighteenth-Century England* (J. Murray, 1951).

British History Online, *Essex*, available at: http://www.british-history.ac.uk/vch/essex/vol9 (accessed 1/10/16).

Castle, Ian, 'Zeppelin Raids, Gothas and Giants', available at http://www.iancastlezeppelin.co.uk (accessed 10/12/16).

Charter 750 (eds), *Saffron Walden 1236–1986* (Charter 750, 1985).

Dickens, Charles, 'Londoners Over the Border', in *Household Words, Vol. XVI* (1857).

Emmison, F.G., *Early Essex Town Meetings* (Phillimore, 1970).

Essex County Council, https://www.essex.gov.uk/AnalyticsReports/CB_LCA_Essex_2002.pdf (accessed 31/10/16).

Essex County Council, 'Unlocking Essex's Past', http://unlock-ingessex.essexcc.gov.uk/uep/custom_pages/home_page.asp?content_page_id=48 (accessed 17/2/17).

Foley, Michael, *Frontline Essex* (The History Press, 2005).

Frinton & Walton Heritage Trust, *Frinton-on-Sea A Brief History and Guide* (2016).

Gordon, Dee, *Essex Land Girls* (The History Press, 2015).

Grant, Raymond, *The Royal Forests of England* (Alan Sutton, 1991).

Green, Georgina, *Keepers, Cockneys & Kitchen Maids* (Geoff Green, 1987).

Grieve, Hilda, *The Great Tide* (Essex Record Office, 1959).

Grieve, Hilda, *The Sleepers and the Shadows* (Essex County Council, 1988).

Hallman, Robert, *Thundersley and Daws Heath – A History* (Summersbooks, 2015).

Higginbotham, Peter, 'Essex Workhouses', http://www.workhouses.org.uk (accessed 17/2/17).

Hill, Tony, *Guns and Gunners at Shoeburyness* (Baron, 1999).

Jones, David, *Chelmsford: A History* (Phillimore, 2003).

Lambert, Bart, and Milan Pajic, 'Drapery in Exile: Edward III, Colchester and the Flemings 1351–1367', in *History*, 99 (338), pp. 733–53 (2014).

London Borough of Barking & Dagenham, 'Dagenham Breach', https://www.lbbd.gov.uk/wp-content/uploads/2014/09/Infosheet36-Dagenham-Breach.pdf (accessed 3/12/16).

London Borough of Havering Education Department, *A Celebration of Havering* (1982).

Macfarlane, Alan (ed.), *The Diary of Ralph Josselin 1616–1683* (Oxford University Press, 1976).

Macfarlane, Alan, *Witchcraft in Tudor and Stuart England* (Routledge, 1999).

Pam, Stephen John, 'Essex Agriculture: Landowners' and Farmers' Responses to Economic Change, 1850–1914', PhD thesis (ProQuest, 2014).

Phillips, Andrew, *Colchester: A History* (Phillimore, 2004).

Poos, Lawrence R., *A Rural Society After the Black Death: Essex 1350–1525* (Cambridge University Press, 2008).

Power, Eileen, *The Paycockes of Coggeshall* (Methuen, 1920).

Read, Julian, 'How Essex Influenced Magna Carta' in *Essex Life* (1 June 2015).

Richardson, T.L., 'Agricultural Wages and the Cost of Living in Essex 1790–1840' in Holderness, B., and M. Turner (eds), *Land, Labour and Agriculture, 1700–1920* (Bloomsbury, 1991).

Rowley, N., *Essex Towns 1540–1640*, Essex Record Office teaching portfolio No. 2 (1979).

Simpson, Alan, *Air Raids on South-West Essex in the Great War* (Pen & Sword, 2015).

Starling, David, *Nice Looking Essex Girls Afloat* (Essex Women's Advisory Group, 2011).

Summers, Andrew, 'Magna Carta in Essex', http://www.essex100.com/magnabook.html (accessed 27/12/16).

Vale, E., *The Mail-Coach Men of the 18th Century* (Cassell, 1960).

Weaver, Leonard T., *The Harwich Story* (Harwich Printing, 1975).

Williams, J., *Leigh-on-Sea: A History* (Phillimore, 2001).

Williams, J., *Wickford: A History* (Phillimore, 2006).

Yearsley, Ian, *Essex Events* (Phillimore, 1999).

INDEX

agriculture 81, 99, 127,
    138, 144–5, 152, 167,
    181
airfields/airports 158–60,
    171–2
Ardleigh 10
Ashingdon, Battle of 23
Audley End 61, 75, 107,
    113, 115-7, 119

Barking 19, 26, 58, 70, 104,
    130–1, 160, 171, 179
Abbey 21, 25, 33, 40, 61
Fishing fleet 127-8
Bartlow Hills 13
Basildon 174-5, 179
Bata, Tilbury 166
Benfleet 22, 36
Billericay 10, 51, 88, 101,
    132, 136, 150, 164, 174
Black Death 49, 52
Blackmore 49, 57, 60, 65

Boudicca 14–15
boundary changes 13,
    178–9
Bradwell 15, 19, 172
Power Station 177–8
Braintree 13, 51, 62, 83,
    99, 117–8, 128, 131–3,
    138, 150, 154-5, 166,
    177, 179
Bright, Edward 102
Brightlingsea 54-55, 106,
    108, 120, 126, 138, 142,
    161
Bronze Age 9–10
Brown, Lancelot
    'Capability' 113–5
Burnham-on-Crouch 168
Butlin's holiday camp
    167–8

Caesaromagus 13, 15
Camulodunum 10–12

canals 107–8
Canewdon 9, 172
Canning Town 140, 160,
   164
Canvey Island 8, 11, 79, 85,
   152, 167, 170
Caroline of Brunswick
   121–2
Chafford Gorge 7
   Cathedral 149, 178
cholera 140–1
Civil War 90-5
Clacton 7, 9, 105, 120–1,
   152, 167–8, 178, 183
Clavering 27, 30, 138
Coggeshall 46, 51, 53–4,
   61, 83, 96
Colchester 7, 10-17, 22,
   25, 30, 34, 36, 41, 42,
   43, 47–9, 51–5, 59, 61–2,
   68, 71–2, 74–5, 78, 85,
   88, 91–3, 99–102, 105–6,
   108, 117, 119, 122–3,
   133, 137–9, 142, 144,
   145, 148, 161–2, 164,
   171, 179
   Colchester Castle 26,
   31–2, 36–7 42, 79, 83,
   94, 96, 97, 110–2
   Colchester Zoo 182
Cornwell, Jack 162–3
Courtauld 129–31
Cressing Temple 35, 51
Crittall, Frank 153–4, 160,
   166
Cromwell, Oliver 57, 90

Dagenham 85, 119, 160,
   165, 168–9, 179
   Breach 103–4
Danes and Vikings 15, 21,
   22–4
De Mandeville, Geoffrey
   28–30, 36-7, 46
De Vere, Earls of Oxford
   28-31, 37, 48, 56, 62,
   74–6, 93
Dedham 87, 100–1, 107,
   182
Dickens, Charles 133, 140
Docklands 104, 139–40,
   164
Domesday Book 30–2
Dunkirk 169–70
Dunmow, Great 13, 37, 47,
   61, 67, 70–2, 117, 158,
   170, 172
Flitch 34
Priory, Little Dunmow 36,
   61

earthquake 142–3
education 62, 68–70, 136–7
Edward VII 148–50
EKCO 173
Elizabeth I 29, 57, 59-60,
   65, 68, 73–8
Elizabeth II 180–1
Essex County Council 58,
   144, 174, 178–9
EU referendum 183

Faulkbourne 101

Felsted 33, 64, 90
Fitzwalter, Robert 36–7
Flemish immigrants 45, 52,
    53, 72, 82, 84, 93
flooding 40, 85, 103, 128
    in 1953 176–7
forests 17, 21, 33, 39–40,
    42, 56, 58, 182
    Epping Forest 10, 18, 39,
    109, 112, 152–3, 170,
    179
Foulness Island 8, 136,
    158–9, 176
Foxearth 139
Frinton-on-Sea 182

Gilberd, William 75
Great Chesterford 13, 15,
    68, 170
Great Stambridge 89, 90,
    107
gunpowder 121, 154, 161

Hadleigh Castle 37–8
Harlow 117, 174, 179, 181
Havering 40, 55 58, 74,
    114, 144, 179
Hawkwood, John 48–49
Hedingham Castle 29–30,
    36–7, 75
Henry VIII 57–62, 68, 73,
    76
housing 41, 147, 164–6,
    174
Hunter, William 71
Hylands House 114

Ice Age 7–8
Iron Age 9–11

Jaywick 167, 176, 181
John, King 36–7, 39

Kelvedon 9, 13, 74, 159,
    172
Knights Templar and
    Hospitaller 34–5

Lakeside Shopping Centre
    182
Land Girls, WWI 161–2
landscape design 113–6
Leigh/Leigh-on-Sea 58, 67,
    98, 102, 105–6, 141, 159,
    169–70
Little Maplestead 35, 59
London 144
    Bishop of 19, 21, 31–2,
    42–3
    boundary changes 179
    trade with 40, 43, 47, 82,
    99, 102, 119, 139
Lucas, Charles 91–3

Magna Carta 36–7
Maldon 17, 26, 34, 52,
    59–60, 65, 68–9, 88–90,
    93, 101–2, 105–7, 133,
    136–7, 144, 150, 179
    Battle of 23–4
    elections 122–4
malaria (ague) 80

Manningtree 51, 94–6, 124, 133, 136
Marconi, Guglielmo 155–6
markets and fairs 15, 40–3, 46–48, 110
market gardening 119
martyrs 71–3
Mary, Queen 58–9, 70–1
Mersea 7, 18, 22, 24, 33, 92, 106, 108, 143, 171, 182
Mildmay family 57, 64, 68–9, 93, 112, 123, 140
militia 73, 90
Morris, William 145
Mountnessing 100, 142

New England, America 88–9
New Hall 57, 74, 91
Newport 46, 59
North Ockendon: Stubbers 84

Ongar 42, 72, 114, 164
oysters 11, 108,

peasants' revolt 50–1
philanthropists 145–6
Pleshey 30, 37, 49, 59
plotlands 167–8
population growth 25–6, 40, 50, 127, 147–8
postal system 101, 124
Purfleet 8, 101,119, 182

Quakers 90, 96–7, 141

Rayleigh 30, 39
Repton, Humphry 114–5
Richard Lord Rich 62–4, 74
Rochford 64, 67, 101, 142, 171–2, 179
Romans 11–17
Romford 47–8, 101, 114, 117, 131–3, 179

Saffron Walden 69, 70–1, 74, 81, 84, 86, 90, 110, 116–8, 141, 144, 164, 178
salt manufacture 10–1, 17, 43
Shoeburyness 9, 11, 15, 22, 134–6, 159, 162
smuggling 104–7
South Woodham Ferrers 179
Southend-on-Sea 10, 21, 108, 121–2, 141, 144, 147, 150–1, 157–60, 164, 169, 170–1, 173, 177–82
St Cedd 19–20
Stansted 27, 30, 37, 180
Steeple Bumpstead 62, 136
Stratford 72–3, 101, 181
Strutt, John 144–5

Tendring 55, 80, 132, 139, 179, 183
Thorndon Hall 113, 161
Thurrock 9, 174, 179, 180, 183
Tilbury 19, 91, 100–1, 119, 134, 166, 171, 181

Fort 76–7
Tiptree 9, 59, 106, 139, 161
Turnpike roads 99–102
Turpin, Dick 109–110

Victoria, Queen 148, 153
Virley 106–7

Waltham Abbey 25–6, 33, 46, 51, 58, 61, 121, 161, 173
Waltham Forest 39, 179

Walton-on-the-Naze 8, 9, 78, 152
Wanstead House 57, 67, 74, 111–4, 179
Wickford 51, 102, 141
Winstanley, Henry 86, 115
Winthrop Fleet 89–90
Witchcraft 77–9, 93–6
Witham 9, 10, 62, 106, 131, 150, 166
Writtle 17, 36, 40, 42, 52, 132, 155–6

Zeppelins 78, 158–9